THE PATH TO A FUTURE

First Edition

www.thepathtoafuture.com

THE PATH TO A FUTURE

First published in July 2009.

ISBN 144146932X

EAN-13 978-1441469328

10 9 8 7 6 5 4 3 2 1

Note to the Reader from the Author

This book is a collection of ideas, thoughts, frameworks, policies and principles. I am not the arbiter of their truth or their value, you are.

Read this book with a critical eye and keep asking yourself if you agree, or maybe you have a different idea, or would adopt a different approach. Make notes in the margins, and discuss them with your friends.

Go to www.ThePathtoAFuture.com and add your point of view to the narrative. We all need to be Path builders, and your ideas are as valid as anyone else's.

Thanks.

Acknowledgement

It is clear that we, as a species, must change in many different ways, and that many good people are working on a myriad different aspects of these changes.

On a deeply personal level, in our relations with each other, ourselves and our alignment with the creation we inhabit, there are essential changes we must make. I honour and empower all the people everywhere who are working to bring about those changes, raise awareness, spread information and support the intention to unleash our potential and reach for our destiny.

This book addresses the realm of politics, the structure of our societies and our economies, and is just one aspect of the many changes we must make.

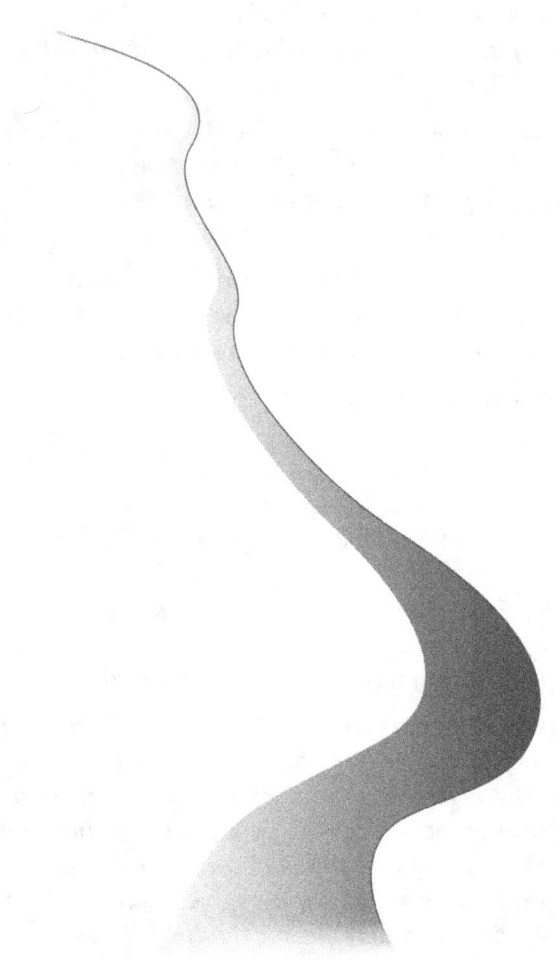

Special thanks to Julia
without whom this book would not have been written

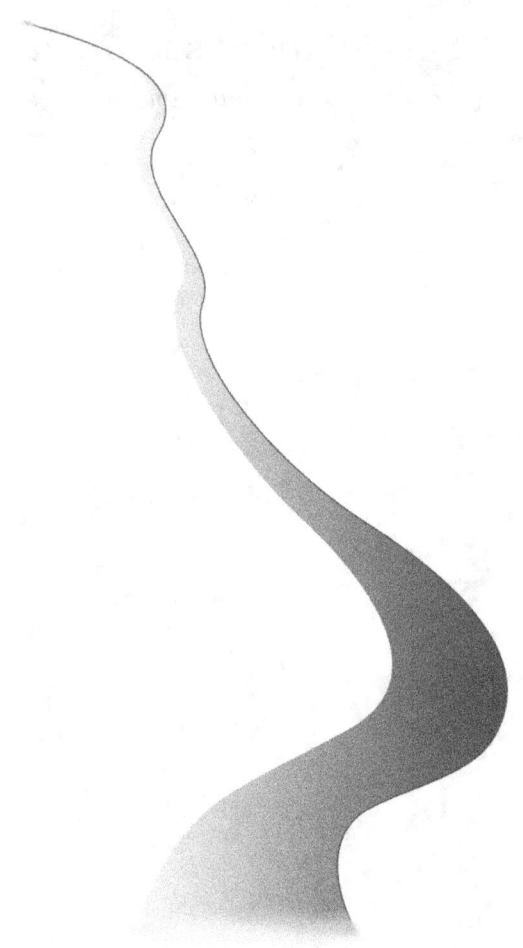

Contents

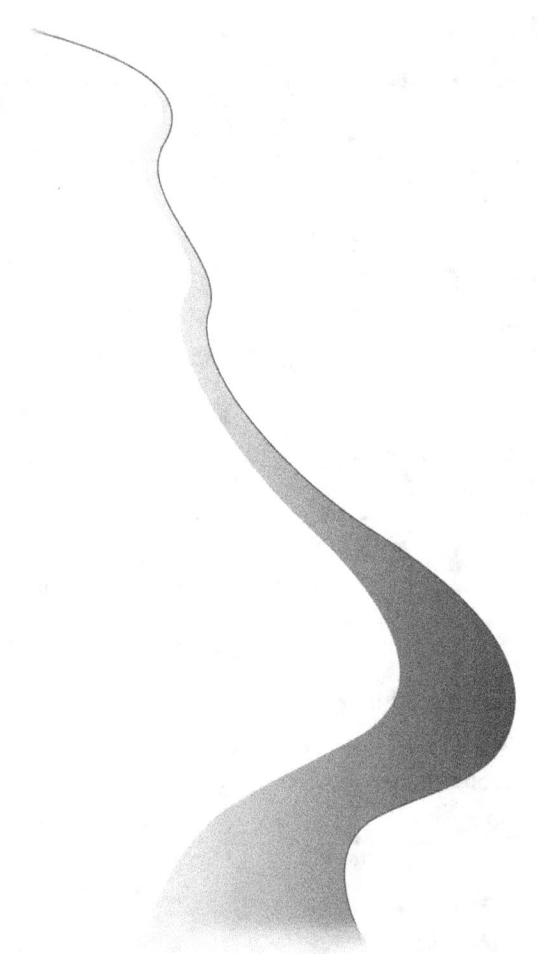

Setting Out

So here we sit on the third rock from the Sun, in an otherwise basically lifeless solar system, living in a gloriously beautiful, paper-thin atmosphere that has the capacity to support and nourish us all. We have copious quantities of energy streaming into and around our planet and the technology to harness it. We have oodles of delicious food and the capacity to grow and distribute it. There is nothing standing between us and global peace.

And yet, as we enter our 41st Millennium, our economies are degrading our atmosphere and pillaging the planet, leaving vast swathes of desolation in our physical and social environments. We are diminishing our capacity to sustain life and are in danger of placing the solutions beyond our reach. Our democracies are perilously dysfunctional, and our grasp of the consequences almost suicidally absent. Only by harnessing our collective wisdom to our course of actions can we make the fundamental changes to our economies and societies necessary to achieve sustainable prosperity.

So, are we really just going to let it all go to ....?

For want of a plan, and the courage to follow it?
Because it requires hard choices and hard work?
Those are not good enough reasons for inaction.

Now is the time to act. Now is the only time we have. Today we can have evolution before revolution, tomorrow maybe not. Change is inevitable, but what changes is up to you and me.

The truth is that there is a path we can take, a path that leads to sustainable prosperity, but we will not choose what we cannot see. We do have the choice. There is a realistic, practical option for coexistence and prosperity. We have only to grasp the opportunity, to understand that this is the right time. This is a time pregnant with potential, and we are the ones alive in this time! All that is required is for us to see a path that will lead us to where we want to go. A clear, simple and achievable path.

Such a path of change must be so rooted in common sense that it is self evident on receipt, and so simple in application that it is realistically achievable by all. It will have to be hewn from the universal nature of humanity, and flexible enough to be shaped by the diaspora that adopts it.

This book shows you that such a path is available.

In the chaos and confusion of these times it seems that we are a little lost as to what to do differently, what to change or how to change it. I am convinced that by starting with simple observation of ourselves we can arrive at a clear understanding of what we need to change, and what it should look like after we've changed it. In these pages I explore natural principles which can guide us in reformulating the structures of our societies. If we start simply and are honest in observing ourselves, we can see these principles at work in our own lives.

Using these principles to formulate a path, we will have a rallying point, a banner around which all who are interested in change can gather together to promote the issues they feel are most important, in concert with everyone else and their individual motivations for seeking change.

This is about getting our act *together*, about focusing on the strategy and channeling our energy and enthusiasm for a better future into a common purpose. Whatever your specific concerns, there is little chance of any of our issues being resolved without a strategic, over-arching framework. We need a construct that serves those that are seeking change, as well as others who don't know what to change, and even those who haven't decided to change anything.

While many futures are available to us, individually and collectively, this is a story about one path that leads to a future in which we live in sustainable prosperity. There are other futures available to us. There are futures full of the same struggles, violence and waste that have characterized much of human history to date. Those futures are indisputably possible, and if we don't choose differently they are our default destination.

The choices we face between peace and war, respect and hubris, love and hate are not new; we have faced them since the dawn of our times. The difference today is that our choices will affect everyone, everywhere, because they will affect the nature of the planet we all live on. Whatever we do, we are headed for massive changes to our cultures and our climate. The difference is whether we choose our own path through those challenges, or wait for chaos to be thrust upon us.

Indeed, the evidence of human history does not support the notion that we will make the choices that will lead us down the path proposed in this book. These choices have been heralded and recommended by our wisest sages over and over again, but rarely adopted and never fulfilled. But they were never as possible as they are now, because for the first time in human history we can truly act globally in unison. As seems uncannily often the case, we are presented with opportunity, at exactly the moment of necessity.

Our religions and our literature have long extolled the value of seeking our higher natures, of reaching for our destiny rather than settling for our fate. We have been told by the wise since the dawn of our ages that love is the manifestation of good in us and that we have the capacity to be the lights in our own creation. However, as a species, we have yet to fashion a working model for this practice. We see the lofty ideals espoused by our sages and prophets as just that: ideals, but not practical solutions. We look around us and see a world full of others who we think will not honour a mutual contract, let alone reach inside themselves for love and peace.

Realizing that appeals to our better natures or our faith in humanity have not proved successful to date, this book lays out a path of action that is intensely practical, realistically achievable and in our self-interest. Rather than asking you to have faith in the primacy of good intentions, this book describes changes that make sense, even if you don't trust your fellow humans to reach for their better natures.

The purpose of writing now about this path is not to promote it as the only option. I, and no doubt you, are only too plainfully aware that we have many options and that we can quite easily follow our fate to our grave, without the courage to reach for our destiny. The reason to write this book, and for you to read it, is to envision a clear path that gives us the chance to choose our destiny.

It is a choice. We have to actively make the choice, if we are to reach a different destination. That means that we have to be able to see the path, to feel it in a very personal way. After you have read this book, I hope that you too will see and feel The Path.

The Path

What makes now such an important time is that we have reached a crossroads. We are at a point where the only constraint on our destination is our choice of direction, our decision to limit our impact on our environment, this planet.

We have scaled the heights of growth and technology so effectively that, without a singular focus on living sustainably, we will change our planet's environment very significantly, probably catastrophically. No matter where you live, or how rich you are, or how clever you are, you cannot be sure that you or your offspring will be amongst the survivors of climate change. Your best bet, by a long shot, is to choose orderly change over chaos. The Path is that orderly change.

The Path follows a simple logic that goes like this:

- In order to bring about the global changes necessary to avoid catastrophic climate change we need peace. Without peace we will not be able to assemble or coordinate the resources and processes required to build The Path to a Future.

- Even with peace, we still need everyone's voluntary, personal and active participation in order to make the right choices, select the best leaders, develop the technologies, work together and implement the changes.

- We're not going to get global peace and cooperation unless there's something in it for everyone. The Path to a Future cannot just be in people's eventual interest; it must be the best thing for each and every one of us to do now.

- Finally, The Path has to lead to a future that we want to live in. The future we aim for must be much better if we are collectively going to make the effort required to get there. This future must not only be sustainable, it must be much more fun, with more freedom and ample opportunities for joy for all.

The Path is made from three simple, reinforcing elements:

- **Peace** is necessary to focus our resources on providing for our security.

- **Security** allows prosperity to flourish.

- **Prosperity** allows us to build greater security that sustains the peace, which makes broader prosperity possible.

These three things are inter-dependant. Not new and not rocket science, but with one big and important difference today: realistic achievability.

The link between peace and prosperity was expressed eloquently by Martin Luther King[1] a generation ago, and the generation before that by Gandhi, and so forth back through the generations of time. What is different now is the global impact of our choices, and the possibility for global change. Before now to imagine globally coordinated or synchronized change was the stuff of dreams, but today the imagined differences and barriers between peoples have been brought low by the advent of global telecommunications.

The fear that others do not want the same results or that different cultures have irreconcilable differences has kept our sights low and our vision narrow. Now we can see on TV, with our own eyes, people in every corner of the world speak of the same desires, the same intentions and the same simple hopes for themselves, their communities and their planet. Mothers in Maharashtra, Manchester and Malawi all want exactly the same things for themselves and their families.

Keep this in mind as you wind your way down The Path with me. It really is possible for people everywhere to adopt the simple changes proposed in this book, and implement them where they live. In our time, in this age, these ideas can be discovered, disseminated and the process of change started. Within a decade change can be happening across the surface of the globe.

---

1   *Beyond Vietnam*, April 4 1967, New York

In this book I will attempt to show you that you can build this Path, that there are changes that you can make in the community, region and state that you live in today. I will try to be explicit about what the changes are, without ignoring the fact that exactly how they are achieved is going to be dependent on your specific situation.

After reading this book I hope that you will share with me:

- A joy about the possibilities in front of us
- An understanding of how the changes work together to create The Path
- A enthusiasm for sharing The Path with others, based on your own intuitions and understanding of its value
- A desire to start the changes where you live

See you on The Path to our Future.

Go online to www.ThePathtoAFuture.com and contribute your perspectives.

7

The Three Premises

Peace, security and prosperity.

The interrelated, mutual dependence of these three factors is the essence of The Path, and we must understand those relationships in some depth if we are to avoid the navigation problems of our past. Tackled independently from each other none of them is attainable, but pursued with a fundamentally integrated vision all of them are achievable.

Peace allows us to focus our efforts and resources on the real problems.

Mutual, universal *security* allows everyone to move beyond survival to become active and voluntary participants in building the Path.

Prosperity is the incentive that draws people to the Path, and it is the reward returned to everyone for building it.

These three premises are inextricably linked, and vital to each other's success.

A context that helps to frame the situation we find ourselves in today arose in the last century with the dawn of the nuclear age, when we ushered in that most human of innovations: Mutually Assured Destruction, or MAD for short. In so doing, we helped to set the groundwork for where we are today: MADDER (Mutually Assured Displacement and Destruction by Environmental Reduction).

Whereas MAD left our fate resting on the decisions and actions of a very few military and political leaders, not going MADDER depends on the decisions and actions of the vast majority of our planet's inhabitants. This necessity for hundreds of billions of decisions drives the course of the Path at every turn. If the Path does not provide for every citizen, every community, every nation, and every continent to join in and travel the same route, it will not lead us to our desired destination. It will only leave us madder.

To get everyone involved, the Path must offer everyone the opportunity to participate in the journey and the destination. The peace, security and prosperity that are the features of the Path must be available to, and attainable by, everyone. I'm sure that peace, security and prosperity are already most people's goals in life, so it is not their desirability but their attainability that is the issue.

This is a very important element that is worth sitting with a while. Any solution, strategy or plan that does not account for the need to motivate and incorporate the vast majority of the world's population into the processes cannot succeed. Good ideas that serve a minority will not result in the level of change necessary to mitigate our planetary impact. The need for universal participation requires that we adhere to serving the greater good of all, if we are to succeed for any of us individually. It's almost as if the universe set up this situation specifically to make us face our most profound choices.

We have spent the last thousand years promoting and establishing mechanisms and behaviours that have led directly to where we are today. We have been so successful in that endeavour that we are now faced with the equal task of disestablishing or diverting those patterns without destabilizing our entire structure. The only way to do this is to make sure that we are following naturally sound principles that serve all the participants, as well as each of us individually.

Peace, security and prosperity are big words, often used by many, and meaning very different things in different contexts. They have quite specific meanings for the Path, so before we go on to explore the relationships between these three premises and their application in our lives, let's get clear about what we mean by each one, individually.

Peace

We're not talking about the global cessation of violence because suddenly everyone has seen the light, and forgiven their neighbors as they would be forgiven themselves. What is necessary for The Path is simply the cessation of violence sufficient to allow those afflicted to stop wasting time, resources, people and technology on destruction. This waste affects everyone around the globe, irrespective of their direct proximity to, or involvement in, the conflict itself.

The causes of conflicts are many, but they can be distilled into fractions of disenfranchisement and ignorance. They are about people having the right and the power to make choices about their own environment. Everywhere you find conflict, you will find one group fighting for their rights and another group fighting to deny them their rights. Quite often, the identity of these groups swings between them over time, as they get caught in the cycle of conflict.

So if enfranchisement and rights are at the root of all conflicts, what are people's rights? What does someone, anyone, have an unassailable, natural right to? The answer is simple: everyone has a right to participate in the decisions that affect them in proportion to all the other people that share the constituency of those decisions. This is the basic format of democracy, and draws its strength and veracity from simple observation of the nature of being a human, living a life.

Starting at the center of each person, standing in the space they are in, it is possible to construct circles (constituencies) that radiate out, like ripples on a pond, to include wider and larger populations of others. In each one of these circles, each person has an equal say as all the others in the same circle.

The way to peace, then, is for there to be a mechanism that abides by the simple truth of every person's rights and allows for the resolution of differences. Such a mechanism would allow individuals to assert their rights in their local environment, without threatening the integrity of a wider circle.

The mechanism to achieve this is representative democracy, except practiced in a vastly more representative manner than we have yet to implement. Our democracies in the modern world are wonderful for what they are, but we need a greatly enhanced version if we are to bring peace to the majority of the world. We need *"super-democracy"*. This advanced, super democratic model has features not found together in any of the versions of democracy being practiced in the world today, although some aspects can be seen in some parts of some modern systems.

The *super-democracy* model is a voluntarily self associating, proportionally representative, multi-layer, directly elected system.

Let's break that down so that we can better understand how it works, starting at the end:

Directly elected: all the citizens vote directly for the same candidates. No electoral colleges and no subdivisions of each circle or constituency.

Multi-layer: every citizen has a direct vote in each constituency of which he or she is a member. Constituencies are geographically defined areas, starting with local communities and stretching all the way up to a global constituency encompassing all the people of the world. A rational model for these layers gives every person a vote in five constituencies: community, region, state, transterritory and world.

Proportionally representative: a vote counting system that provides equal weight to every voter's vote, in proportion to the other voters in that constituency.

Voluntarily self associating: each constituency is empowered to choose its association with the constituency that contains it. For example, a Community can choose to belong to any Region with which it is geographically contiguous. The same goes for Regions and States.

The combination of these attributes into a coherent political model empowers people to take responsibility for themselves, and then build on that to resolve their differences with their neighbours. This form of *super-democracy* has the power to mutate conflict into disagreement, and from there to allow the motivation of self interest to drive future cooperation and progress.

This model is not just for people in conflict areas, everyone needs to be availed of the benefits of *super-democracy*. You will see as we travel The Path that it is vitally important that we have a properly representative system to support our decision making. Its exemplary adoption by those of us already living in relative peace is vitally important to the movement of the world's conflicts from violent destruction to negotiated disputes within the short time available to us.

By establishing a mechanism that allows people to have control over their immediate environment, and yet be part of larger and larger entities, *super-democracy* removes the need for the larger constituencies to impose their identity on their members. At the same time, it provides the smallest communities the right to self-determination without threatening their neighbours. The simple process of allowing self-determination to coexist within structures that also provide for harmonization, is the key to peace and is the power of *super-democracy*. Its structure allows those in conflict to work their own way out, at their own pace, and based on their own self interests.

Conflict comes from inside those involved in it, and the peace has to come from them too. However, conflict also tends to deprive people and their communities of the resources and infrastructure necessary to support the administration of democracy, which makes moving out of a cycle of conflict all the more difficult. Those external to the conflict can help by providing guidance, process, structure, facilitation and support to the afflicted as they replace conflict with democracy. Because the administrative infrastructure for *super-democracy* is not geographically or culturally dependent, generic training systems, voting systems, technology and legislative bureaucracy packages can be developed for rapid deployment anywhere in the world.

So the first building block on our Path is *super-democracy*. A building material sufficiently robust to be used in the roughest parts of our landscape, and yet flexible enough to accommodate the particular topology of different situations. A simple, yet malleable, foundation for peace on our Path.

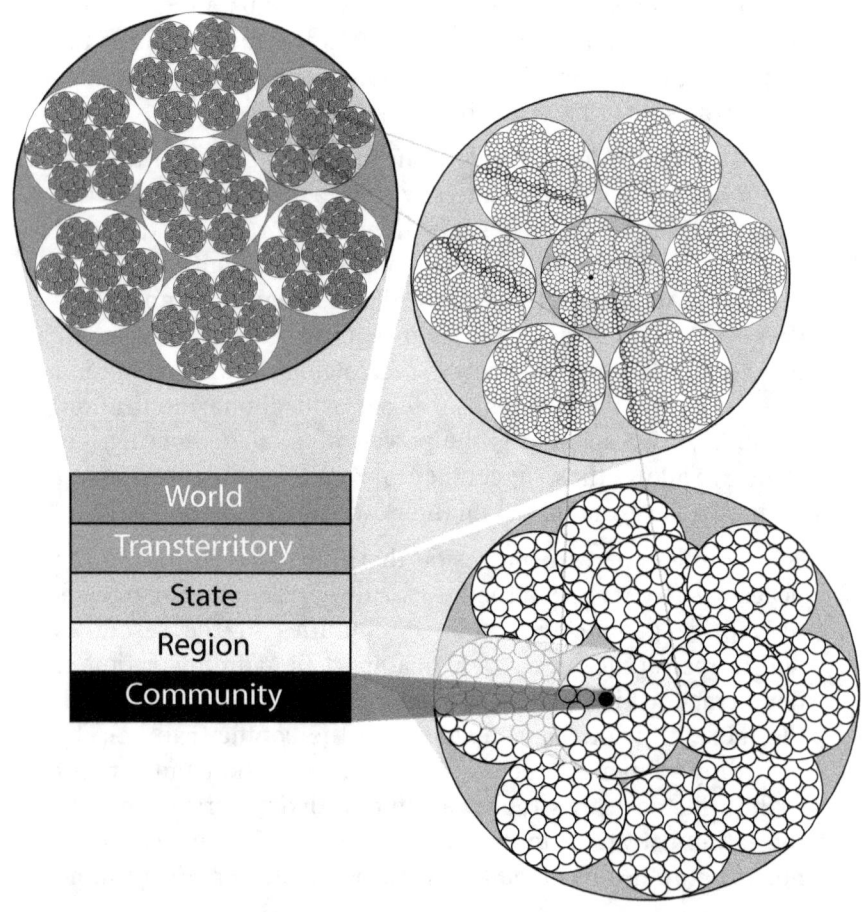

World
Transterritory
State
Region
Community

Security

To reach our destination we need the full participation and maximum contribution of every person. When we talk about security on The Path to a Future, what we mean is the personal, material security of each person. Our personal participation requires that we are not wondering where our next meal will come from, or if we will have a roof over our heads when we get too old to build a house. If people are insecure about their own futures, they will not lift their sights enough to act in the best interests of everyone and the planet.

Population control, mutual cooperation and environmental management are all dependant on the personal security of each and every person in the world. The cessation of violence and focused attention on transitioning to sustainable economies are also dependent on the personal security of people everywhere. So personal security is a vital component of our Path.

To provide this security, every society will need to provide every member with the bare necessitates of life as a right of citizenship. Everybody needs to be freed from basic need; this is not the same as free from want.

We're not talking about 20th Century social security benefits here; we're talking about a 21st Century personal security underpinning for the whole society, what we will call "*super-security*".

No cash, just services.

The security we need must come from a mutual guarantee to each other that, no matter what fortune befalls us, we will each ensure that the other has the bare necessities for life, and the opportunity to make what we can of our circumstances. Of course, the extent, breath and quality of the services will depend on the capacity of the particular constituency we live in.

At the most basic level, shelter and sustenance must be guaranteed globally, to all, at every age. Fully implemented, personal security services include healthcare, education, transport and information. These services need to be provided free of payment, at the point of need and universally to every citizen and resident of the constituency, without means testing.

This concept of personal security is, at once, so simple and so shocking. We tell ourselves that of course we wouldn't step over the bodies of those less fortunate than us as we walk down the street; but we also tell ourselves that we cannot possibly provide everyone with free food and shelter. We think we can't afford it, and that it would cause our whole system of commerce and labor to disintegrate.

The reality is that we can afford to do it, it's not expensive and it creates the platform on which to build the most productive society that human history has ever known!

A same basic rate of income taxes we pay today of between 25% and 30% will fund these services, in full, in the average industrialized society. The mechanism that makes providing personal security affordable is linking the costs of the services directly to the tax system; such that an average earner is paying sufficient taxes to pay for the services they receive. Many of us in those societies already pay those rates of taxation (federal, state, local, social security and health insurance), without receiving the benefits of the personal security that could be provided!

Guaranteed basic personal security does not destroy incentives. We all know for ourselves that as soon as our most basic needs are met, our next level of desires arises, and those are every bit as strong an incentive to all of us. The difference is that in the pursuit of our higher needs we make our more valuable and unique contributions, greatly enriching the fabric of our societies, far beyond the desultory contributions we make for mere survival.

As we move forward to describe other aspects of The Path, just keep in mind that we need the maximum contribution and the full participation of everyone, if we're going to make it to our destination. The personal *"super-security"* of everyone is the key to unlocking the energy and focus we need to build The Path.

Prosperity

That brings us to the third premise of The Path: prosperity. Prosperity is a mixture of wealth, peace and freedom that delivers a high standard of life. It is a natural human ambition to aspire to increased prosperity; a natural outcome of the combination of our instinct for survival, and our desire for relief from hardship.

The challenge is to reconcile this natural inclination, with the sustainability of our actions to attain it. Prosperity for the minority, at great cost to the planet, is plainly possible for a short time. We have already achieved that, but sustainable it is not. Not only is our current path to minority prosperity environmentally unsustainable, it is also socially unsustainable.

We need a new economic vision for our future. The prosperity we create going forward must be environmentally and socially sustainable, and to do that it must be resilient to the cycles of monetary systems and resistant to the vagaries of climate change. That requires us to move beyond mastering the crude art of industrial-scale extraction, to develop the finer skills of production with reduction, recycling, renewables and, above all, sustainable resilience.

Many thanks to Amory Lovins, Rocky Mountain Institute, for the following definition of resilience, as it so well describes the economy and prosperity we must build:

"An inherently resilient system should include many relatively small, fine-grained elements, dispersed in space, each having a low cost of failure. These substitutable components should be richly interconnected by short, redundant links. Failed components or links should be promptly detected, isolated, and repaired.

Components need to be so organized that each element can interconnect with the rest at will but stand alone at need, and that each successive level of function is little affected by failures or substitutions at a subordinate level. Systems should be designed so that any failures are slow and graceful.

Components, finally, should be understandable, maintainable, reproducible at a variety of scales, capable of rapid evolution, and societally compatible."

A finely grained, richly inter-connected economy made of many small parts that are understandable, maintainable and societally compatible. Such a micro-economy can satisfy the desires of prosperity and sustainability concurrently.

There is enormous prosperity potential latent in our societies today. The time has come to extend the opportunity to contribute at our highest capacity to the entirety of our populations. The development of communications technologies in particular, but also transport, engineering, miniaturization and alternative energy technologies, have opened the way to pluralistic economic development on a scale that was not possible before now.

These advances in technologies allow us to leverage the unique skills, interests and capabilities of people everywhere to create a rich fabric of micro enterprise that compliments and balances our industrial enterprises. There are as many unfilled needs in a day as there are people on the planet, and somewhere there is someone ready and willing to produce the product or service that will fill each one of those needs. This is the prosperity potential of our planet. If we can unleash even a fraction of that potential, we will easily generate the wealth necessary to power our societies along the Path to sustainable prosperity for all.

The two keys to unlocking this latent potential are:

- development of micro market places
- free availability of human resources

Marketplaces are essential to the development of prosperity, and modern communications technology creates the possibility for markets in which every person can offer their unique contributions to meet the needs of others. The reason that the congregation of people in cities has been a hallmark of our historical prosperity development, is because cities enabled marketplaces. Now we have the capability to create location-independent marketplaces in the virtual world, for products and services in the real world. We need systems that can connect the billions of needs with the billions of producers, locally and transnationally, through fluid marketplaces that allow the natural ingenuity and innovation of the human spirit to flourish.

To a certain extent, this has already started with the advent of the Internet and the appearance of market services such as eBay and craigslist. What is needed now is a set of trans-global marketplace standards that will enable different markets all over the world to interact. This flourishing of micro-economic activity will be intensely local, but it is vital that each local market can exchange with its neighbours. The barriers of language and culture are not going to go away anytime soon, and the cost of transport is only likely to rise in the future, but trade will remain a vital aspect of our economies. So a rich fabric of geographically specific local marketplaces need to be the hubs around which networks of regional and transterritorial marketplaces rotate.

Small businesses have always been the largest employers in our economies, and the backbone of our social fabrics. Now we have the opportunity to extend the chance to be self-employed to everyone, because we can provide the marketing, technical and social support necessary.

Removing barriers to micro-enterprise is also necessary. Many tax regimes and social support systems today create "poverty traps" that actually discourage people from using their skills and capacity to build their own livelihoods. That will be completely resolved by implementing *super-security*.

In addition to the marketplace mechanisms, people need to be free to participate in them. That freedom is a function of the peace and security of the society, and requires that we build the structures and services that support them. We all need to be delivering our maximum individual contribution to the greatest extent possible, and that means having the *super-security* that allows us to live above the level of survival or subsistence.

Prosperity is the fruit of the tree, and it springs naturally from the branches of well nourished and protected populations. Lots of people using their unique and personal talents to create products and services that can be sold and bought through micro-enterprise markets. That is the engine of sustainable prosperity! That is a *super-economy*.

The diverse and diffuse nature of micro-economic activity makes it vastly more resilient to the ebb and flow of particular markets and economic cycles. It also has the potential to generate significant wealth, because the growth of wealth is largely driven by the volume of value-generating transactions in an economy. The liberation of micro-economic potential has an explosive capacity to exponentially increase transaction volumes.

This is the "*super-economy*" of our future, and it needs the personal security that will enable us to contribute at our highest capacity, as well as the marketplaces in which to find the needs for our contributions. If we provide these, our individual and collective prosperity will flourish gloriously.

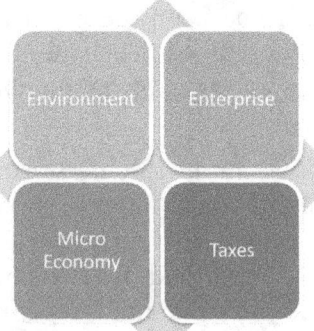

Platting the Super-Trio

So there you have The Path: a new democracy, real personal security and a micro economy. No barriers to their implementation save for our own decisions to do so, especially if led by the 'developed' world.

To use the same language that you will see repeated later in this book, the term *"super-trio"* refers to the presence of all three of these primary elements of The Path: *super-democracy*, *super-security* and a *super-economy*.

There is a great deal of synergy between these three aspects of The Path, and in many ways they are interdependent. For instance, the promises of micro-economic inspired prosperity will not bear fruit without universal personal security. Embedded in the required precursors for the new democracy, are the freedoms and protections that will enable the new economy to leverage technology fully, as is necessary for marketplace development. The new democracy is dependent on the promises of security and prosperity to stimulate the effort required to make the changes that are necessary. It's all intertwined.

Although one inevitably wants to start somewhere, all of these processes are interdependent and it is important that we make progress in all aspects of The Path as soon as we can. If we can harness personal security before we have the chance to change the democratic structure, we should do so. If we can start introducing digital marketplaces for micro needs, we should not wait for personal security to arrive first. We don't have a lot of time, and every small aspect of the path that comes into being supports the rest of its development.

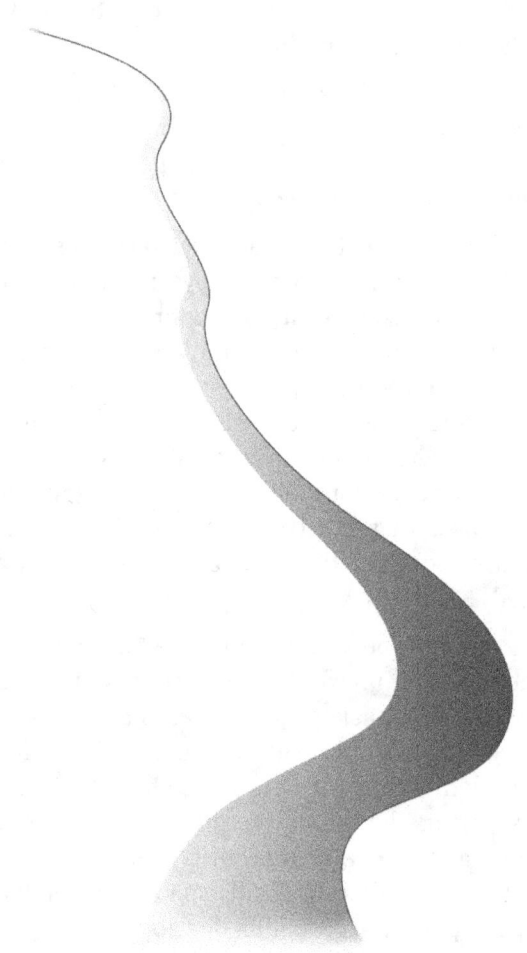

It's personal, this time...

I realize that it's a personal moment, it's just my time to stop hoping, to stop waiting. Don't get me wrong, I have replaced hope with intention, waiting with action. This is a positive moment for me.

I'm not angry. After all, until I reached this moment I was a contributing member of the lethargic, hopeful establishment. I was waiting for other good people to come out and make a difference. I was hoping that a little better and a different emphasis was going to lead to something. Hopeful that change was just around the corner.

Now I know. Now I'm satisfied that tinkering incrementalism and insider knowledge are not the keys to change. Now I can skip the mini-steps that I had hoped would lead to the big stride, and go straight for the stride.

I no longer look at the moderate candidate that just beat the really extreme candidate, and breathe a sigh of relief. Now I know; they're not really going to change anything anyway.

They were brought up in that house, they know that house well, and they live in that house. To them, redecorating the inside and repainting the front door are big changes that will require lots of work, coordination and coalition building.

I'm out the front door and past the garden gate, and I can see for myself that I want a different house.

When I see all the public support for change, I see people asking for new houses. Maybe that's just wishful thinking, but I now know that I've always wanted a different house. I also used to think that redecorating the old house would somehow magically make it different.

Now I know. It won't. I'm building a new one.

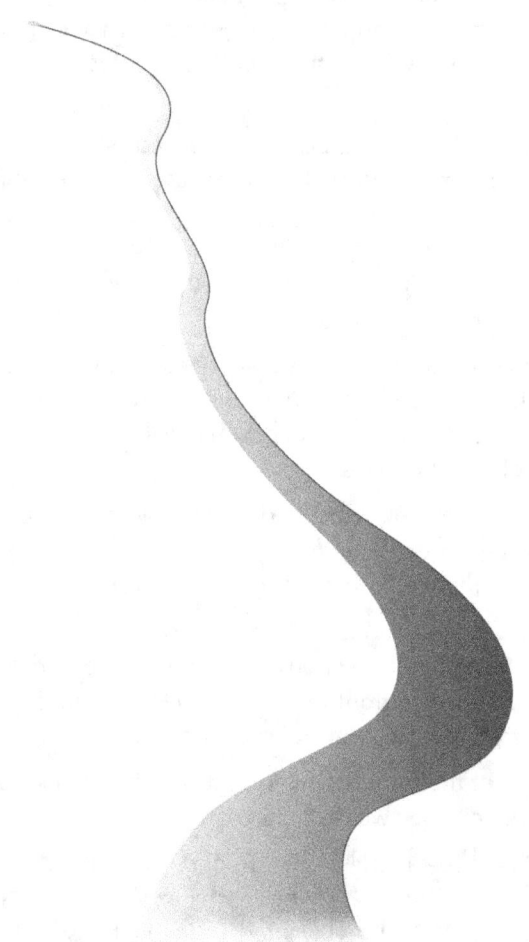

The Landscape of the Path

Before we build our Path we should understand the nature of the landscape we intend to cross: the state of the world today. We need a clear view of reality, so we can determine the line our Path should take.

We live in a world that is still ravaged by many conflicts, and where the disparities between wasteful over-consumers and the desperately poor grow wider every year. For all our good intentions, we are not living within the bounds of the resources available to us; and the vast majority are not free to enjoy the passage of their lives in peace and security.

The good news is that we do not have to achieve the impossible to remedy our situation – we will not have to fix *everything*. We do have to change the way we organize our societies and the structure of our economies, and we have to change them pretty fundamentally. Along the way we are going to be challenged, distracted and tempted by our attachments to old ways of doing things. But making fundamental changes, and staying the course through difficult times, are the hallmarks of our greatest moments. Our ability to be flexible and resolute in the face of adversity are natural features of the human landscape, and therefore of you too.

The Path to a Future is all about finding a way from where we are today to a prosperous, sustainable and peaceful future. The Path will not remake the landscape as we find it, it must negotiate the landscape as it is; and that includes us as we are.

Some of the greatest barriers we will have to cross are our own assumptions about what is possible, about what others will do and about what we really think is important. To get started down The Path we're going to have to open our own gates, step out and get a clear, fresh view of the landscape.

Take a walk with me and let's have a look at the lay of the land. Using the analogy of a physical landscape, we can examine the contours of our cultural and emotional world. We can get some perspective on the challenges we face, and assess the most effective way through them.

The Valleys of Conflict

One of the most recognizable features of our landscape today are the valleys of conflict that cuts across the view, trapping people and resources into separated schisms covered by whirling fog. These are the conflicts which obsess our headline writers and dominate our news. They are not most people's everyday experience of life, but they obscure our view and add so much to the difficulty of navigating across the land that we have no choice but to build the bridges necessary to unite the different sides. We must bring the light of day to all those enured in conflicts, so they can see the view from the outsides of their chasms.

Conflict entraps all those who are touched by it, innocent or not, perpetrator or victim; they are compelled to look in instead of out. The irony is that many of these valleys were dug out purposefully, by some group expecting to improve their view by placing another group out of sight. Not unnaturally, those forced into the valley resist and start to climb out, at which point the original creators of the valley return to dig wider and deeper, until they find themselves living in the same valley with those they sought to displace.

While conflicts originate with an intention to hoard resources, they act like valleys and inevitably develop watersheds that divert resources from all around to flow down their course. The resources (approximately $3,000,000 a minute as of the time of writing this) consumed in conflicts are stolen from their better uses, be they people or materials, ideas or energy, they have been diverted from their alternative application.

Whatever their origins, we must clear the fog and build the steps that will allow those inside and outside the valleys of conflict to look up and move forward.

The Mountains of Tradition

Towering over the landscape we can also see the great icy peaks of mountains formed out of the chance encounter of great land masses, rising up faster than the natural forces of erosion can soften their edges. Their peaks are cold because they rise up to where the air is thin, and the clouds gather around their shoulders to obscure their view of the land beneath.

It is in the nature of mountains that they are unaware of their shadows, as they bask in the light that strikes them. The taller they grow, the more inhospitable their peaks become; places from which the beauty and gentleness of the land below becomes almost impossible to recall. They find their identity in the height of their tops. They are jealous of neighbors and oblivious to the violent weather, freezing temperatures and thinning air that surrounds their highest accomplishments.

Beheld from a distance their majesty is clear to see, but up close their inhospitability is keenly felt. Unaware of the simple fortune that created them, and their final destiny as the sand on the shore, they are both dividers of lands and peoples as well as bringers of rain and nourishment.

These mountains represent institutions and traditions of every kind; from the monolithic mega corporation to giant government departments, from established religions to superstitions and legacies laced through every culture. They started with a useful purpose and many still serve valuable roles in our societies, so it is better that we see them for what they are, acknowledge them and then move on.

In navigating the Path, the mountains of tradition are better skirted than summited, tunneled than toppled and appreciated than admonished. For they know not of their origins, their shadows or their value, they know only of their height and the weight of their ice.

The Quagmires of Morality

The most dangerous of the landscape features that need to be navigated are the bogs and swamps of the lowlands. These seemingly flat and vegetated expenses are the premature terminus of many a journey.

Offering the delusion of easy passage, their self-reflecting pools and slippery sod are the perfect traps for fools. Seen from a distance they show neither the steep ascent of mountain ridges nor the obvious cut of valley grooves, and would seem to represent a clear distinction between the hubris of the high and the laments of the low. In reality, these are the mosh pits of morality.

Quagmires are the places where we lose sight of our real purpose, and get caught up in the attempt to assert our moral standards over and on to others. Being right is not the objective, getting to our destination is.

Without delving into moral judgments about morality, let's consider what happens when attempting to cross a quagmire: you get bogged down. Endless effort is expounded in simply moving from one pit to the next, and soon the entire endeavor becomes focused on navigating the swamp; forgetting that there is a destination beyond there.

Path building is an intensely practical task and there is much ground to be covered. It is a service to all beings on the planet and does not discriminate between opinions; we have neither the luxury of time, nor the surplus resources, to engage with matters less practical than reaching our goal of sustainable prosperity.

Because we often have difficulty identifying quagmires from a distance, we must develop our sensitivity for recognizing when we are entering one. As soon as we find the ground shifting beneath us, we must turn and seek the firm ground that surrounds the swamp. Don't worry, there is always another way; a course for The Path that is lit by the lamp of freedom.

Landscape Lessons

So what can we glean from this brief review of the features we must navigate on our path?

- First, all those features do exist and must be navigated. We cannot wish them away.

- Second, they have formed naturally. That is to say that they represent some basically natural aspect of our collective makeup that we must individually own up to. They are not aberrations that we can dismiss as unfortunate. They are simply possibilities that we can seek to exclude from our future, by choosing different aspects of our nature. The difficulty of our passage through them can, and should, serve as a reminder to us about ourselves.

- Third, they are unavoidable and natural, so it behooves us to seek a path that is in harmony with the landscape, which takes advantage of the natural slopes and shelters in the coves eked out by the passage of time. The Path must get across the landscape in order to deliver us to our final destination, and it serves no one to make the journey about flattening mountains or filling valleys. Passage is the password and having built the Path, it will allow everyone to travel along it, from wherever they are now.

In summary, there are three aspects of the world we live in that our path of change has to accommodate: conflict, traditions and morality. These are all reflections of perfectly natural aspects of our human nature, and to fight against them is both futile and fatally distracting.

We have to remember that our purpose is to reach our destination. To do that we need only define a path that navigates the landscape. We need conflicts to be calmed, to reduce their senseless waste. We can allow traditions to fill their role, so long as they do not stifle progress. Morality can continue judging, if it is not harming. To do other than these is to try to change our natures, and that is not the purpose of The Path. The goal of The Path is to show us the way to a sustainable and prosperous future, with all our imperfections unremedied.

So if we're not going to change these features, what will we do about all the people who have come to identify with them?

Carry on building.

When The Path is mapped all the way to its destination, when they can see the value of the destination and the holistic coherence of its route; their aspirations will trump their old attachments and they will travel with us on the same road.

Fear not!

There is a path across this landscape.

We can determine its course, and we can build it.

Congruity

Congruity, [*con-gru-ity*] : simultaneous, mutual reinforcement
in proximity and extremity.

Congruity is our word used to describe the process of building The Path. It symbolizes the unification, interdependence and broad reach that our actions must have, because although we can accurately describe The Path as linear, going from peace to security to sustainable prosperity, we will have to embark on all these processes concurrently.

The reasons for this are twofold: we are short on time, and each step reinforces the others.

We are really short on time! We've probably got a decade to get the ball rolling, a decade to get processes up to speed and a decade to spread the changes across the globe. Even once we are on The Path, we will be leaning on advances we will have made just to cope with the wrenching climate changes that will still come our way over the next half century or more. If we can't get the ball rolling in the next ten years, then we run the very real risk that the changes being forced upon us by then will drive people to reaction, and the opportunity to promote our common good will narrow or even fade completely.

The second reason for congruity is the corollary of why attempts at peace have failed in the past. Peaceful people in the past, particularly prosperous and peaceful people, have been subjected to the crude interruption of the brutally violent. The reason for this was because the prosperous and peaceful were unable to spread the benefits of their prosperity to those others. If we are to succeed on our Path to A Future, we will have to bring rapid change to as broad an audience as possible, as fast as possible and to spread the benefits as widely as possible. Partly because we are all dependant on each other's actions as we inhabit a single biosphere, and also because our path must travel through peaceful lands, it cannot be built with fences.

As we explore the practical applications of The Path you will see that the elements that make up The Path are interdependent. Peace is a critical element, without peace we cannot afford to secure our social fabric and our personal security is necessary to liberate our prosperity. All of these processes reinforce each other.

On The Path, not only must these congruous processes happen in one place at one time, they must spill over to impact the lives and societies of others at the same time.

That is "congruity".

Two Words about the Destination

Sustainable prosperity.

It's a simple description that will not get embellished much in the course of this book, hopefully because it is self explanatory. But it is worth taking a moment to clarify what is not included in that description.

- It is not utopian.

- It does not suggest equality of outcome.

- It does not speak to the veracity or ascendancy of any particular worldview beyond the simple context inherent in the word "sustainable".

- It does not include any necessary configuration of peoples or places, nor does it to accord credence to a situation based on the history that led to the way it is now.

- It is not a guaranteed or self-fulfilling prophecy; it will require choices and work all the way there, on arrival, and thereafter.

- 'Prosperity' is intentionally modified by the adjective 'Sustainable'.

What the destination is, is wedded to practical outcomes in the natural world and it is, above all, realistically achievable.

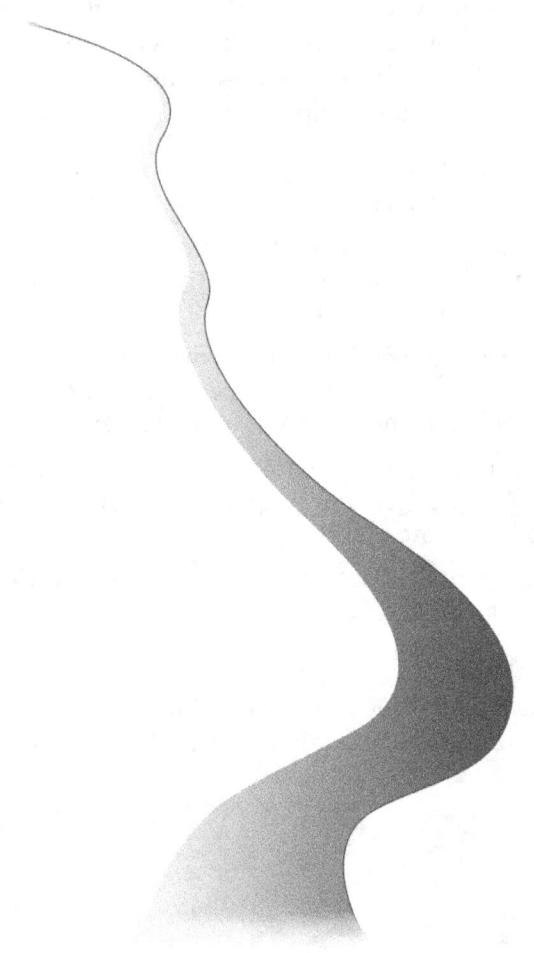

The Great Gamble

*This chapter is for you if you question the need
for change. If you don't see why we should make
fundamental changes to our societies, our economies and
our democracies read on.*

*If you already know that fundamental change is necessary,
you can skip this; or read it to help yourself understand
why others don't see things the way you do - enjoy.*

We, as a species, are engaged in the greatest gamble of our brief existence. The outcome will affect all of us, but not everyone has a place at the table nor is everyone playing with the same hand.

The gamble we are taking is embodied in two questions. Questions we have to answer if we are to consider ourselves masters of our own destiny.

- Do we need to change the fundamental structures of our societies and our economies to avoid catastrophe?

- If we do, when do we need to start making those changes?

The easiest answer to both questions is that we do not have to make any fundamental changes, that peace and prosperity will be ours without changing anything very much. This answer demands the least from us and would seem to have the least impact on us, assuming the answer is the correct one.

For the majority of this world's inhabitants, that answer would be inconceivable. Most people can see their environment changing, their water being polluted or disappearing, their crops yielding less, their opportunities diminishing and their freedom out of reach. They do not live in peace and prosperity today, and they know that something's got to change fundamentally if they or their children are going to have any chance of either peace or prosperity.

If you live in peace and prosperity today, you probably live in the "developed" world or are a member of the ruling elite of any nation. If this describes you, then you are sitting at the table and you are taking the gamble; you are a card player. As the lucky recipient of peace and prosperity today, you have the greatest stake in and influence over everyone's peace and prosperity. Your fate, your peace and your prosperity are the bets on the table, and you are doing the gambling.

If your answer is that nothing substantial needs to change, then doing nothing is a bet that will pay off. But if fundamental change is necessary to protect your peace and prosperity, and if the necessary changes are going to take a few decades to effect, then doing nothing today is a very poor strategy. The risks of being wrong go up every day, as the odds of being able to make the changes in time go down.

"Doing nothing" encompasses a range of different positions and actions, all of which are the equivalent of doing nothing, because they waste time not making changes.

Doing nothing includes trying to prop up or resurrect the status quo; it may feel like action and it may look like action, but it isn't making the necessary changes; so it's the same as doing nothing.

Fatalistic abstinence is doing nothing. Deciding that nothing can be changed is a self-fulfilling prophecy. It is a failure to be here now, to live in the place that you exist in. You'll never know if action could have changed things if you don't act. Predicting dire futures that are rescued by the indeterminate resurrection of some amorphous possibility may be a satisfying justification for inaction, but it is still doing nothing.

Doing nothing includes going about your day doing lots of things, being busy and accomplishing the goals you have set yourself. But if you don't change anything, if you don't see a need for change or aren't supporting change, then you are doing nothing too.

In the face of mounting evidence that something needs to change, doing nothing, in all its guises, is supported by two arguments: we can do something later, and doing something now will be just as deleterious as doing nothing. These arguments are only relevant if you're on top of the heap today, a card player sitting at the table.

The risk of leaving change for tomorrow is that you need to have an accurate notion of how long it will take for changes to take effect, and of how much time is available. If it takes longer to make the changes, or if the time available is shorter than you expect, it will be too late. So if your bet is that change can be forestalled, then you better have a really good grasp of how long it will take to implement the changes required, and how long you've got to complete them in. Your risks are compounded by the fact that neither of these variables are really knowable with any degree of certainty. Fundamental changes to the world's societies could take decades to complete, and there's a big difference between two decades and five decades. The impact and timing of climate change are also unknowable; we can have a good guess, but the planet is a massively complex system with a myriad of feedback loops. So a strategy of wait and see is extremely risky, because there's no way of knowing whether waiting even one more year will be too long. You just can't tell, and the downside of being wrong is that it is a game loser. Betting on this option is the equivalent of putting all your money on one number, for a single spin of a 1,000,000 slot roulette wheel.

The other reason to do nothing is that you are doing so well right now, that virtually any change is bound to reduce your prosperity, your security or your advantage. You may be tempted by the advantage you have today, to feel that under almost any circumstances you're better off without fundamental change. The political leadership class of virtually every society in the world falls into this group, and that represents a serious obstacle to change. These are the high rollers at the table, the players with the most to lose and the most cards in their hands.

These high-stakes players are crucial determinants of how the game will play out. There are two factors that can influence how they act: control, and mutual results.

In a democracy, these high rollers are there by the choice of the people they represent; if the electorate develops a different view of how important fundamental change is, they can replace the players with other representatives who will act for change. The same replacement process can happen in societies that don't have democracy; it just tends to be bloodier and messier.

The probability of mutual results could also influence those high rollers that retain their political control. Mutual results is the reality that however the game plays out, we are all affected in the same way, in the end. The high stakes players and the lowest stakes players will all experience the consequences of getting it wrong. If fundamental changes are needed and not enacted in time, the resulting chaos and destruction will affect everyone everywhere on the planet; no matter how rich, how clever or how remote they are.

Mutual results may influence the big players, but it may not. It may seem to them that the odds of a negative outcome are not as bad as they appear to be for the vast majority of other people. In this situation, wresting control away from them will be key to our mutual survival.

A big part of this gamble is the assessment of risk. To stand a reasonable chance of a life lived with peace and prosperity, we are going to need to make accurate and clearheaded calculations about the odds of success for any course of action we take. There are risks inherent in the decision to make fundamental changes to our societies, but the odds lean towards a favorable outcome for the vast majority of us. If we start making the right changes now and we're too late, we won't have lost anything. Probably the biggest risk we run is that we make the wrong changes and exacerbate our problems. But if we focus on improving our decision-making processes while reducing the environmental impact of our economies, the chances are good that we're doing the right things anyway. Nevertheless, what to change and how to change them are very important things to get right; and that's what this book addresses.

So we have a high-stakes game in which our chances of living in peace and prosperity, maybe even our survival, is at play. The game is mostly being played by a few of the people in the room, and even amongst the players there are those with significantly more cards in their hand. Everyone in the room wins or loses together. The cards represent changes we can make. We can keep them close to our chest, only putting out the minimum number we need to keep the game going; or we can play big, put down a royal flush and go for it. Because everyone wins together, the royal flush strategy has very little downside, but it does mean that the pot will have to be divided amongst all those present in the room. The alternative of a cautious game, favors the players who are at the table, because they don't have to share their stakes while they have them on the table and the game is still going on.

The risk is that the game will end without anyone playing their winning hand, and everyone in the room loses.

So if the game clock says that there are about five more minutes left to play, what would prevent the players at the table from putting down the strongest straight in their hand?

This is where we are. This is the risk we are running.

We, the players, have to look hard at the clock, and ask ourselves if we really think it's too early to play our strongest hand.

Apparently, we haven't decided to play our hand yet. Apparently, we still think there's time and that it serves us to keep our cards for now. I say this because we have not collectively summoned the will to align our actions with a different outcome. We are still on basically the same path and the same trajectory that we have been for the last 100 years: industrial growth that will 'float all boats'. That's the equivalent of keeping all our cards in our hand and if we're wrong: we're screwed, along with everybody else. Just in case that is the wrong strategy, let's look at the facts of our situation and review the state of our game today.

Are we relying on our instincts to make the right choices for survival? Are we making choices today that will deliver the results we want tomorrow? These are important questions if we are betting our lives on them. Never mind doing the right thing, have we fundamentally miscalculated the odds? Have we even calculated the odds at all? If not, we could be making a dooming mistake on an evolutionary scale.

In our daily lives we routinely select making better choices tomorrow, in favor of easier choices today. We select personal safety, over the rights of others. We select not looking, over knowing. We select the safety of established opinions, over the dangers of an open mind. We select how it was, over how it could be. We select low price, without recognizing the unincorporated violence embedded in that price. We select personal enrichment today, over the consequences for others tomorrow. In most cases we don't really think about the choices we are making, our gut tells us that these are the right choices. But are they?

We have a hard time choosing between peace and money. You probably don't think of it that way, but many of our conundrums can, and should be, expressed as peace versus money. We equate money with security, and that is the phraseology we consciously use to justify and rationalize our choices. We say to ourselves that we are choosing security, not money.

We accord money with the equivalence of security because of a gut level instinct that money should bring us personal security from hunger, hardship and deprivation. This is quite likely true for many of us in the short run, but we would do well to note that our real desire is for security with peace, not the money itself. The money is the means that we believe will enable us to create the security which will allow us to live in peace. We actually desire peace, it's just that we believe money will give us peace.

We are attracted by the notion that we can own money, that we can possess and protect our money. Whereas peace is not a tangible asset. We understand that peace exists only in the moment of time, dependent on our mutual intention that it should.

When we choose money over peace we do so because it seems more likely to reach us personally than the notion of peace, which we are dependent on others to attain. We choose money over peace when we support oppressive regimes for access to minerals. We choose money over peace when we buy products made from those minerals. We choose money over peace when we make drugs illegal, and buy them anyway. We choose money over peace when we begrudge paying taxes to help others. We choose money over peace when we build more prisons. In every case we argue that our aim is our security. What we mean is our personal security, a very close and narrow view of our personal security, right here and now. The security of our supplies, the security of our morality, the security of our low prices and the security of our lifestyles.

But we are not choosing peace.

We really do desire peace, but we do not actually choose it. We know that helping to oppress the freedom of others is not a choice for peace. We know that poverty does not foster peace in our communities. We know that locking people up does not lift them up. We know all of this, and yet we still choose money over peace. And guess what? Our choices beget our rationale. The oppression, the poverty and the violence that we create, and now see all around us, are further fodder for justifying our decisions to choose money over peace. What d'ya know? Whodathunkit? Our inward facing, narrow, personal logic (aka instinct) has led us to create exactly what we feared all along.

But we still want peace. That hasn't changed. All the money in the world is no good to us if it does not bring us the security of peace. We know that too. On some level we know that we are taking the great gamble. We are gambling that the personal security we purchase, will last the longer than it will take for the un-peaceful consequences of our choices to catch up with us.

We know that the unfree will seek freedom, that the impoverished will seek their own security and that the put down will rise up. We know all this because we know that that is what we would do if we were there. So we can even see the circular counter-logic of our own arguments, but we still choose money over peace. We are engaged in the risk-reward gamble that has defined our evolution, and which is a fundamental, natural part of our most basic makeup; what we call our "gut instinct". A set of animal reflexes designed to ensure survival from one moment to the next.

So let's work with this a little. We choose money over peace because our basic instinct tells us that money is a safer bet than peace. The reward of security bought with money now, feels like a safer bet than the risk that peace will become unattainable where we live, within our lifetimes. We are betting that the wars will happen somewhere else. The poor will not steal from our kitchen to feed their children, and that if they try that we will be able to lock them up and put them away. We are betting that the wars and the poor can be kept at bay, at home and abroad.

If we have got this wrong, the consequences of our choices will destroy our peace before we can experience our purchased security. That would be a mistake that money would be unable to redeem for us. A cool-headed evaluation of the odds is necessary here, before we simply accept our assumptions

Perhaps one of the first and easiest rationales that comes into our heads, is that we are simply doing what anyone else would do. But even if we can argue that everyone else would make the same choice, that isn't really relevant, because it is only those of us that have the opportunity to make the choices that are actually defining the consequences. It may be true that others would do the same, but we are the ones making the choices and taking the gamble. It is our choices that are actually determining the outcome. Besides which, mutual poverty of rectitude is not an assessment of risk; it's just an excuse for inaction.

So let's evaluate the three primary mechanisms that we believe tilt the odds in favor of money being the right choice for us. Those are:

- any consequence of war or conflict will not visit us personally,
- the poverty of others will not directly affect our lives
- we can erect a system of legal protection, that will insulate us from any risks that escape from the first two assumptions.

Wars will Stay Over There

That wars will stay over there, is the first part of our gamble. Certainly this used to be true, but increasingly we can glimpse the chinks in this armor. We call it "terrorism", and it is abhorrent to target civilians, but we would be well served to recognize that to others it is the globalization of freedom fighting. The same technologies and facilities that smooth the flow of modern commerce are being used by the disenfranchised and the oppressed to spread war outside the pretty confines we would prefer them to stay within. Terrorism is the last resort of the ignorant freedom fighter, but maybe we should figure out that when we see terrorism, it means that some people may have reached their last resort. It would seem pretty obvious to conclude that suicide bombing is the very last resort of anyone, and if we dismiss it as merely the act of a lunatic, then we are not making a cool-headed assessment of the situation. The reality is that war is now mobile, it will not stay over there.

Your own intuition, and every security professional in the world, will tell you that you cannot prevent the manifestation of terrorism, you have to act on its root causes. On the whole we can keep the affects of remote conflicts out of our everyday lives with ever more secure border controls. But the risk that they will spill into our lives through any one of countless opportunities for disruption, from hijacking our transport to poisoning our food supply, is very real. Even if we can keep the actual wars away, can we keep the violence out of our lives?

The Poor can be Kept at Bay

This is the second factor in our calculations of the odds for our gamble. Implicit to this is the acknowledgment that there are poor people; so it is not the existence of poverty that is our risk metric, it's our ability to mitigate the impact of *their* poverty on *our* lives. Fundamental to this calculation is the ability to "manage" poverty. That is to say: to control the depth of the poverty, and the location of the poor. If the poor aren't actually starving, if they have at least something left to lose, then they are less likely to be a threat to our security. Also if they aren't close to us, the less of a risk they pose to our security, however deep their poverty is. So keeping the really destitute as far away as possible, and the poor that are closest to us out of total despair, would seem to be the tricks to maintaining the odds in our favor. Or, to put it the other way around, the risks are: that the really poor will come over here, and we will not sustain sufficient hope in our local poor.

Of course this gets a little difficult, because the more we help our local poor, the more attractive it becomes for the remote poor to move closer. Even this is manageable, if we can stop the poor from moving around. The trouble with that is that really poor people, denied the ability to improve their situation where they live, tend towards migration and revolt. Those feed into the aforementioned terrorism and war problem; which is another relationship we will have to factor in, when making our final calculations.

So "managing" poverty is a little more complicated than it might appear to be at first. There is no doubt that the local poor represent the most immediate threat to our security, so we have to make sure that we use some of our money to keep them at bay. We can improve our odds if we can keep them from starvation, hold out an advertisement of opportunity and, at the same time, keep their life expectancy low. Just enough support to keep bellies full of cheap food, just enough glitz and glamour to provide the illusion of opportunity, mixed with low levels of education and healthcare to keep their actual ability for progression to a minimum. This formula to create a "happy poor" has worked pretty well for the last hundred years, but it is not actually new. The Romans, the Mayans, the Egyptians, the Ottomans, the English and the French have all given this strategy a jolly good go in the past. The trouble with it, as a stand-alone risk mitigation strategy, is that it doesn't deal with population growth; poor people have a tendency to have lots of children, as a means of increasing their personal security. Unless you can reduce the average life expectancy of the happy poor below the age of reproduction, you can't stop their numbers growing. The more of them there are, the more of your money you have to spend on keeping them happy. Sooner or later the balance is going to tip, so you won't have enough left to buy your own security because you're spending too much keeping the poor happy. Past attempts at fixing this conundrum have included sending the poor off to die in wars before they can reproduce, or sending them off to reproduce abroad in colonies. The former has reduced potential nowadays on account of prohibitions against using children in the military, something that wasn't a problem anywhere only a hundred years ago. The latter is problematic today due to the lack of places left to colonize. So the risks posed by local poor are more difficult to mitigate these days and, to make matters worse, we have to face the fact that any version of "happy poor" has its limitations; because even modest levels of education and healthcare are going to result in larger populations and higher demands.

The Law will Protect Us

This brings us to the third risk mitigation factor in our calculation: legal restraint. If we can't get the poor to voluntarily restrain themselves from rudely interrupting our purchased security, we can always try using a legal system to control their unsociable activities. We can increase the odds of our successful use of money to buy personal peace, if we use some of our money to keep the most troublesome poor out of circulation. When we can't keep them away or happy, then we can lock them up. On paper this looks like a reasonable strategy, but it has some real problems that limit its effectiveness. First and foremost amongst these is that it requires that we pervert the natural course of justice; the consequences of this have an insidious inclination to detrimentally affect the quality of our own peace and security over time. If we are to use the legal system to keep the poor down or out, we have to develop a legal structure that specifically discriminates against the poor. It has to target crimes that the poor are more likely to commit, and attach penalties to those crimes that are sufficiently punitive to keep the guilty effectively repressed. To support those two objectives, it will have to include a legal process that ensures high rates of conviction by suppressing the poor's ability to use the system to defend themselves.

Now, while those are all well and good on their own, and we have shown that they are perfectly possible to enact, they include a fundamentally unbalancing consequence that bodes ill for our overall odds: they don't make the poor happy. While we are trying to suppress the top tier of troublemakers, we are actually increasing the dissatisfaction of the great majority of the rest of the poor. Again, this is only a risk factor and it can be managed by upping the quantities of cheap food and distracting illusions of opportunity. But it does have its limits, and sooner or later you reach the point where you just can't afford to keep putting poor people away, and down, at the same time. It all costs money, especially putting people away – it's far cheaper to kill them, but that avenue is increasingly closed as a realistic option, especially in large quantities.

So how do the odds look now? What are the chances that our choices to buy personal security with money will outrun the consequences of selecting against peace? I'd say that the odds look a little short, and they look to be getting shorter every day. Obviously it has worked in spurts over time, but we live in a different world today where the opportunity to mitigate the risks is very different than it used to be, and even those opportunities that do still exist have very definite time constraints. Populations are growing, weapons are proliferating and people are starting to evaluate the quality of law against the justice that it delivers.

It really comes down to time. There's obviously a fuse on this stick, and the gamble comes down to how long you think it's going to take to burn down. Is that enough time to make choosing money over peace now the right choice for you? And even if it's the right choice for you today, how long will that remain the case? Do you perceive that at some point in the future the scales will tip, and it simply will not be possible to buy personal security while ignoring the consequences for peace around you? If you do think that that time will come, when will that be? Next year? What about a decade from now, or when your children are grown? And then how will the transition happen, when the odds flip the other way? What will be the consequences of your choices today, when the time comes that those are no longer the right choices? Will the consequences of today's decisions magically evaporate as soon as you start making different choices? I think not. Right? I mean, you are still the same person and you did make those prior choices, and you could reasonably be held personally responsible for having previously chosen money over peace. Even if you aren't held personally responsible, French Revolution style, you will still experience the consequences, unless you're dead.

So how long is that fuse? This is the heart of the gamble. For how much longer is it going to be the right choice to have selected money as the option that delivers you the rewards, and when will it become the choice that only compounds the risks and blows oxygen on the sizzling fuse? I would argue that that time has already passed, but I am obviously in a minority, albeit an increasingly large one, on this matter. I think that every day we continue choosing money over peace we exacerbate the situation. We sponsor more wars, we create more poverty and increase the violence of our societies through oppression, subjugation and deprivation.

Now let's throw in a relatively new factor: global climate change. Again, this is possibly subject to a discussion about timing, but its reality is no longer the subject of debate. What climate change does, is throw all of this into stark contrast. Not only are many of the historical avenues for mitigation already closed, now the pressures on our global society are going to increase from every angle. Climate change directly and negatively impacts all the significant factors used in calculating the odds of money being the right choice over peace. Climate change puts pressure on resources, increases the likelihood of mass migration, and these in turn increase the likelihood of war, poverty and erosion of the rule of law.

Given that climate change, by itself, threatens peace everywhere; what does that do to the odds for making decisions that further reduce peace in the world right now? It makes matters worser, faster. I think climate change changes everything. The time scale for the impacts of climate change are short; maybe a decade, maybe five, but anyway you look at it, they fall into the bucket of now. Now, because we all know that having chosen money over peace for centuries, it is not going to be reversed in a few months, or even a few years. The consequences of our past choices are going to take decades to be mitigated, let alone stopped. Reversal could take many decades. We know this, it doesn't take a brainiac to figure out that getting to peace, from where we are today, is going to be a lot of work and take quite a lot of time. The harder we work at it now, the less time it will take; but it's still going to take some time. This is relevant, because if it's going to take, let's say, 30 years to move our societies onto a peaceful footing (the equivalent of extinguishing the fuse) then we, personally, have to start choosing peace over money 30 years before the flame reaches the stick.

Here's the choice we face today: will we extinguish the fuse before it reaches the dynamite? Will we figure out that the odds have changed and that choosing money over peace today is the wrong choice? Can we see that we are almost at the point where it is no longer a question of risk that we are making the wrong choice? We are entering a time when it is a certainty that peace over money is the only survival choice we have. If we can't lift our heads up for long enough to look out over the landscape of our consequences and discern the changed nature of our times, in time, then we will let the fuse burn down and the stick will ignite. Our wildest fantasies of greatest dread will pale in comparison to the reality of the times after that event.

I, for one, am for extinguishing the fuse, turning the corner, recognizing the reality of the odds, and choosing peace over money now. There are those, I know, who would say it's too late, that we have already passed the moment when the fuse was extinguishable; and now there is naught that we can do, save prepare for the explosion. I am not one of those. I can see a different future. I want to gamble now that choosing peace today is the right choice, the survival strategy, the best chance I have. That is the gamble I want to take. I choose peace over money, and I choose to do that now.

If you're serious about choosing peace, then the next question has to be: how do we get there from here? What do we need to change and what are we aiming for? Those are the questions addressed in this book. A path that leads from where we are now, to where we want to be. It's not for the faint hearted and it requires that you have decided to choose peace; but if you have, it provides a map for changing the world.

You take your first step, and we can go the rest of the way together.

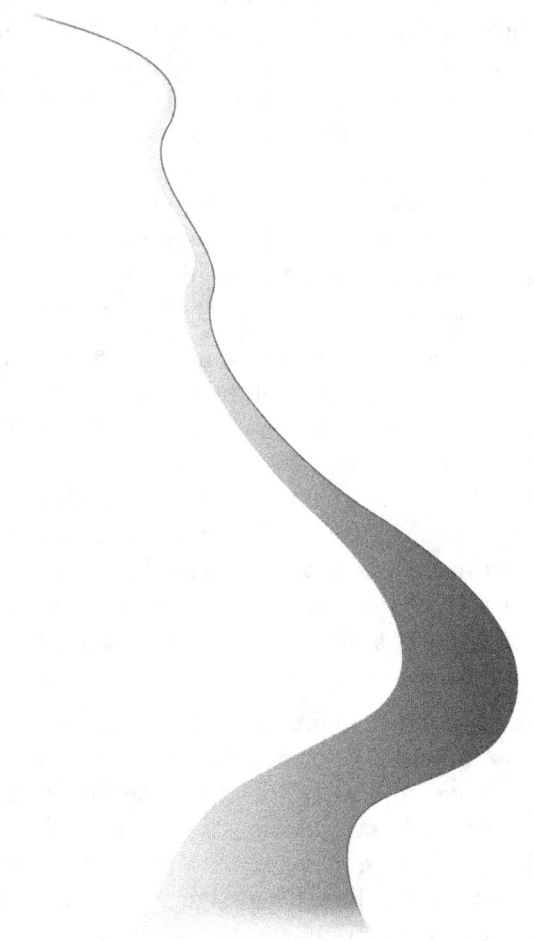

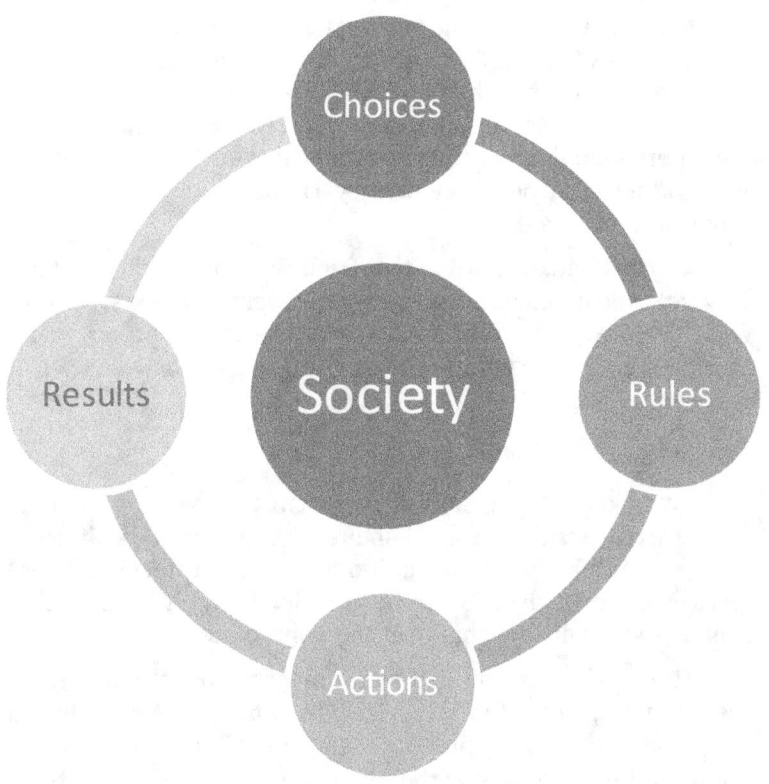

The Standards of LIFE

The Standards of LIFE *are a set of constructs that make the super-trio a reality in our personal and public lives. This briefest of reviews will help set the stage for what you are about to read.*

Peace

A universal Constitution creates a democratic structure based on five layers of government, starting with local Communities and building up to include everyone in the World. A system of proportional representation ensures equal voice for every person in the constituencies they live in. The Constitution also codifies the personal privacy rights of every citizen as superior to the state.

All laws and authority stem from the Community and are only voluntarily passed up to higher layers using a system of Variable Law. Communities can retrieve their authority and change their membership of their containing constituencies at will.

Security

Every citizen can access supporting services that meet the bare necessities of life: shelter, sustenance, healthcare, transport, education, information and legal protection. These services are provided, as can be afforded by their Community, equally to all, without charge at the point of need.

The services are funded by a universal income tax that is used only to pay for those services. Income taxes are collected at the highest layer practical and distributed directly to Communities who control their expenditure.

Prosperity

Enabling micro-enterprise by leveraging technology to develop marketplaces allows sustainable prosperity to flourish, powered by human ingenuity.

Environmental protection is enhanced by pricing in Nature's externalities at every practical level.

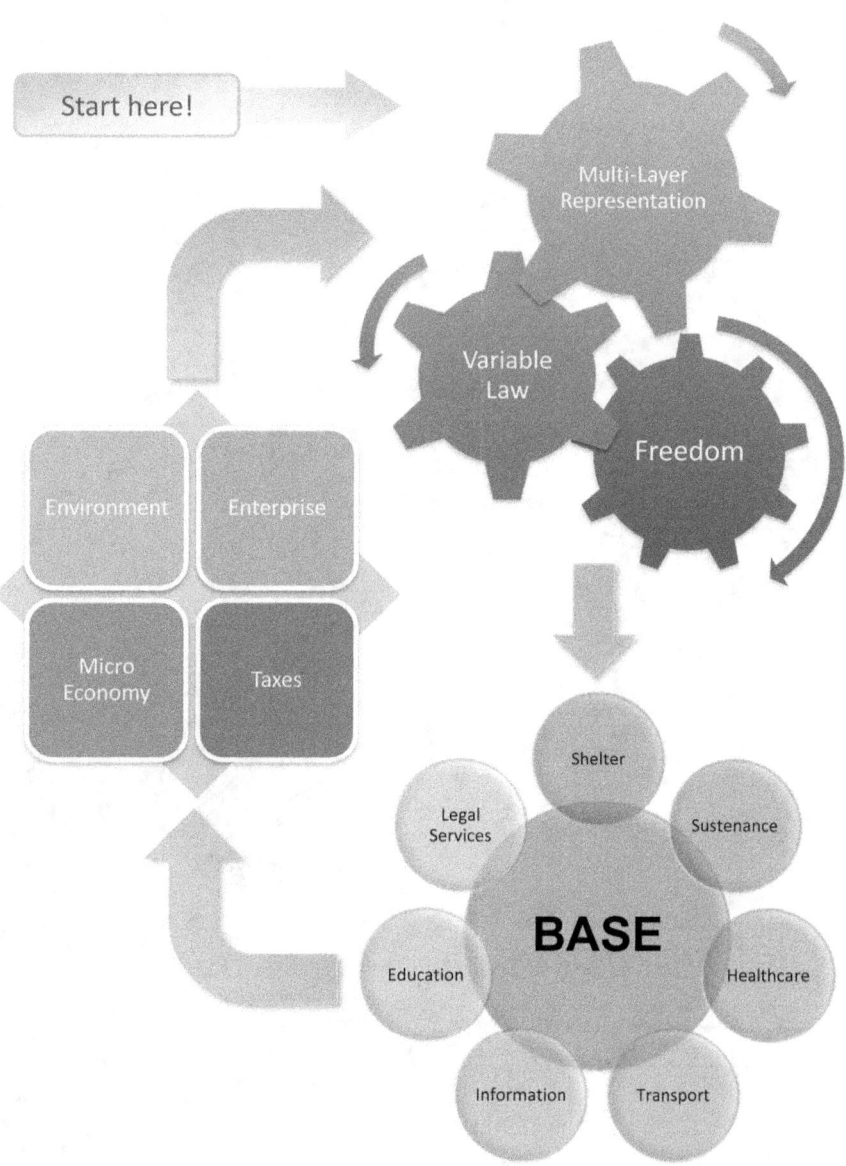

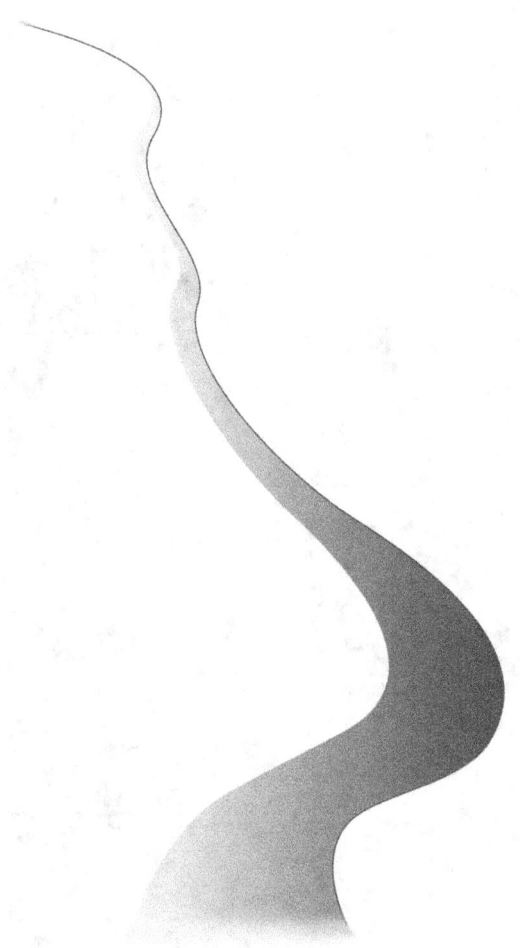

Mapping the Real World

In this section of the book we will visit some of the topics of the day to see how the *super-trio,* embodied in The Standards of LIFE, maps The Path through these issues, and provides realistic solutions to these real-world problems.

We will step out of philosophical discussion, into the intensely practical questions and issues that we face in constructing The Path. Creating our future requires that we come to terms with the very real issues we face today. We must exercise our imaginations and develop our vision, if we are to see through the fog of our everyday existences and map a route for our Path. Working through these examples and issues develops our understanding of the difficulties and challenges we face.

The subjects have not been arranged in any particular order, and in reviewing each one of them it is not my intention to detail every aspect of The Path. You will be able to see for yourself how the different parts of The Path weave together to create a holistic framework. If you find yourself needing more detail, please go online to the web site at www.StandardsofLife.com where the principles, standards and policies are explained in detail and at length. I have yet to encounter a real world situation that the Standards of LIFE do not naturally address, but the details of their application are constantly being refined and extended as they are tested against real circumstances.

You can read through these scenarios one after the other or just pick the subject areas or titles that most interest you. Either way, please rejoin me in the final part of this book to explore the orderly changes we all need to start our journey along The Path.

Economics 001

The economy, and implicitly the development of wealth, is a core issue that too often suffocates the debate about our options for change. Many of us come to the table with assumptions about the relationship between wealth and prosperity. We need to re-evaluate these assumptions if we are to develop solutions to our problems. In this section we will revisit the basic constructs of economics and wealth creation, to make sure we are operating from a realistic and accurate foundation when we formulate the framework for our economies.

The typical policy debate today is about the balance between the social ills of the free market, and economic ills of a state-controlled economy. This suggests a built-in assumption that we must compromise our social security to let markets be free.

Why is that true? Why is it that market freedom is a function of social insecurity? What is it about economic theory that stipulates a need for the population to be prepared to pay a piece of their personal freedom, in order to get to a piece of the market freedom pie? The conventional answer to this is that the labor force needs an incentive to work, and that sometimes the appropriate incentive is survival. Apparently, without the threat of destitution, people will not take the jobs on offer in a free market!

Which leads to the next question: why would a free market create work that only those threatened with starvation would want to perform?

Oh I see, a free market doesn't necessarily create undesirable jobs, it's just that the free market rewards low cost, and low cost means work and reward conditions that only the potentially destitute would agree to work in.

Right?

This cyclical assumption that low cost requires undesirable work, which demands an insecure workforce, is fairly deeply embedded in our current cultural psychology, especially in the West. In fact it isn't really challenged, because it is so widely held and so subtly integrated.

As I will show, the opposite is actually true. Secure populations, working voluntarily in jobs of their choosing, is the most productive economic model available. The "market" is not a policy model, it's only a mechanism; it is no more an economic, or political, model than the explosion in a cylinder is a car.

Our desired outcome is prosperity. That is the destination everyone understands we are aiming for; everything else is just a means of achieving prosperity. The free market is not the destination, any more than collective bargaining is. So the first link to unhinge in our minds is that the "free market" is what we need. Keep your eyes on the prize: prosperity.

The "market" is a set of mechanisms that naturally directs resources to meet needs. While its principles are simple, in operation it accommodates a bewildering array of inputs, influences and outcomes. It's like our brains: we know the principles on which they work, but that doesn't mean we know how to work them.

Cost is a significant input to market mechanisms. When all else is equal, cost drives decisions to the most efficient outcome; that is the raison d'être of the market. But we should note that, almost always, cost is the last criteria in the decision tree; the item has to be fit for purpose first, and affordable second.

What about trade? Within a given market, does the locality need to be the lowest cost producer of the good or service? If trade is possible the answer is no, because if equal and lower cost items are available through trade, then trade will fill the need. Unless... unless the item is so vital to the survival of the population or the basic functioning of the society, that a breakdown of trade, for any reason, would be a strategic threat to everyone. There are certain items that are so strategically important that higher cost is not a barrier to local production, and the market must necessarily be modified in order to accommodate the higher priced, locally secured items.

This leads us to an important place on our journey and we would do well to stop and clearly annunciate our conclusions:

- The market is a great system for almost everything.
- The market is not an appropriate mechanism for the most important things.

> *Whoa! How did we get here? I'm a free-market capitalist and I've been around for a while so I know a thing or two about the world I live in, and this doesn't sound right at all! I'm going to have to go back and read those last few pages again. You've used some crazy commie logic to trap me into believing that the free market won't solve these problems. Wait here while I reread.*
> ...
> *Okay, back again. Well, um, I can't see where I could disagree. It's not like it's complicated, right? There's just some stuff in the world that's too important to outsource. I can see that.*

Thanks.

Now the other news: if there is no strategic imperative, there's no reason to interfere in markets. This is where some get caught up in a different false linkage: they think that we can intervene in markets to make them produce social welfare and justice. In fact, the basic social welfare of our societies is not an output of markets. Markets do not have "well-being" as an output in any of their functional logic. Markets efficiently direct resources to fill the needs of consumers, that is all they do. The welfare of society and our quality of life have to be outputs of human endeavor, they are a function of choice. We do not have to choose the common good or a high quality of life, and we certainly won't get either if we wait for markets to deliver them.

Let's be fair to markets while we're here: they don't know how to benefit society, and it's extremely unfair to ask them to do so. Markets, especially those catalyzed by modern banking systems, are good at creating wealth; but wealth is not the same as prosperity. Prosperity is a mixture of wealth, peace and freedom that delivers a high standard of life. So if we want prosperity, we have to mix the output of markets, with the output of our choices to promote peace and freedom.

When we can clearly see these distinctions, and the properly differentiated roles for economics and politics, we can formulate more coherent policies that are more likely to deliver our intended outcomes.

Economic policy should concern itself with:

- the maintenance of markets
- the management of the monetary system
- the administration of strategic resources

Political and social policy should focus on:

- the cessation of hostilities
- the protection of liberty
- the general welfare of society

Let's look at each of these policy areas in turn, so that we may more clearly demarcate their boundaries. Once we have separated them in our minds, we will be better able to act in the right places to produce our desired results.

Economic Policy

The maintenance of markets involves trying to ensure that they function as freely as possible by correcting naturally occurring defects as much as is possible. The two most common defects in market function are the imperfect distribution of information and the exclusion of external costs.

- Making as much information as possible available to consumers, with the lowest barriers to acquisition, is the best we can hope for; you can take a consumer to information, but you can't make them know.

- External costs, "externalities" in official parlance, are those costs that can be directly attributed to the lifecycle of a product or service, but for which there is no one to demand payment during that lifecycle. Nature is a good example of a non-payment-demanding party to many transactions. When these externalities are recognized, the proper maintenance of market function requires that these costs are imposed on behalf of the non-payment-demanders, usually in the form of some kind of tax, duty or other loading of the item's cost profile.

The management of the monetary system is primarily about preserving the value of the currency. Given that there is no real basis of tangible value in a modern currency unit, it is important that the quantity of money in circulation be managed in line with the output of the economy. Furthermore it is essential that the banking system charged with the care of private deposits, debts and equity be regulated for stability. Modern economies based on monetary systems require a trusted banking function in order to operate, and so the maintenance of that system's stability is paramount. (Banking is entirely different than investment management, which is not really a banking function at all, and should be kept separate from banking. In fact, the term 'investment bank' should be abolished.)

The third leg of economic policy is the administration of strategic resources. As discussed earlier, there are resources that are so important to the sustenance of a society that trade cannot be relied on for their procurement and distribution. These resources must be identified and their supply purposefully managed, such that their availability is as guaranteed as it is possible to achieve. Chief amongst these resources are shelter, food, healthcare, education, transport, energy, information and the legal infrastructure of democracy (the same services that form *super-security*). In most situations only a subset of the total market for each of these resources is strategic, and only that subset need be the subject of public policy. For example, the availability of clean drinking water is a matter for public policy but this does not need to extend to the bottled water market. Similarly the provisioning of primary health care as a public service, does not preclude the availability of specialized procedures in the private market.

Those are the elements of economic policy and maybe you've noticed certain absences that you might normally expect to be part of contemporary policy portfolios. Before going further, let's do a quick review of the complementary political policies that accompany our economic policies, to shed some light on those absences.

Political Policy

We have said already that political policy should concern itself with the establishment of peace, the protection of freedom and the provision of welfare. As regards the economy, the establishment of peace and the rule of law are precursors to enterprise and trade. The freedom of the people is necessary for proper market function, the development of business and the fostering of innovation. Indeed, the freedom to choose and the freedom to fail are essential to the fluidity and effectiveness of market mechanisms.

The provision of public welfare is commonly understood to be the primary function of government, but the policy framework to deliver effective results has eluded most, if not all, to date. Public welfare policy has been colored by our history and has yet to free itself from the shackles of our legacy perspective. During the last century or so we have developed levels of efficiency and productivity that have created the capacity to provide universal welfare. The capability of the population to sustain itself, without reliance on the grandesse of a ruling elite or the magnanimity of magnates, means that we can truly deliver the bare necessities of life to all, at a reasonable cost to all.

The cost of universal shelter, sustenance, healthcare, education, transport, information and democratic freedom is about one third of the total output of modern economies. That's right, for about 30 cents on the dollar we can afford basic housing, a healthy diet, primary health care, reasonable education, local public transport and universal digital information access for everyone. Not everyone is going to want or need every service, but if they did, we can afford to provide them today; with the same tax rates we are already paying.

So why aren't we doing it? The primary reason goes back to the starting premise of this section: the idea that the provision of such welfare would fatally undermine the economy, the very system that produces the wealth that makes it all possible. And we're back to the same logic we questioned at the start. Do we believe that the motivation to work, to innovate and to be more productive will disappear if we aren't afraid of starving to death in the gutter? This is not reality. It misunderstands human nature, and the meaning of "welfare".

Human nature is full of aspiration; that is what has driven our development over time. Once we have filled our bellies we desire taste; once we have rested we desire comfort; once we have seen color we desire lights and once we are satisfied we wish to contribute. The religions of the world are the ultimate examples of our capacity for aspiration, far beyond the mundane practicalities of life. Providing a roof, a bed and a bowl of soup does not satisfy the aspirations of anyone. Would it satisfy you? Wouldn't you still want to see a movie, eat some chocolate or wear different clothes? Perhaps you'd rather own a mountain bike, become a photographer or grow some vegetables? To believe that providing the bare necessities of life to someone will blunt their motivation and dull their aspirations, is to negate what you know about yourself. It's simply not a reality, not of anyone, anywhere.

So what should public "welfare" policy actually provide? The policy should aim to satisfy a basic, mutual social contract between neighbors: ***that no matter what fortune befalls you, you will have the bare necessities of life, and as much opportunity to make the most of your life as can be afforded***. Viewed in this light, welfare policy is not a benefit that anyone is entitled to, it is a service delivered to the best of their neighbor's ability.

Public welfare policy is really about delivering personal security and opportunity. As such it does not involve the transfer of payments, instead it delivers services that fulfill the social contract. Housing is made available to provide secure shelter, food sufficient to maintain health and medical services as can be afforded for all. Think of them as services, not dependent on the largess of some individual or group, but provided universally, as a birth right of citizenship. No cash, no luxuries and only what can be universally afforded from a reasonable tax.

Now start to imagine the impact of such a public welfare system on the economic system. No need for a minimum wage. Everyone has their basic sustenance taken care of, so they are free to provide or pay for labor at whatever rate they choose. On almost every level required for a flourishing market economy the situation is improved: workforce mobility, propensity for risk, innovation capacity, skills development, productivity, confidence and satisfaction. The implementation of universal personal security will have a dramatically beneficial impact on economic output, at the same time that it enables "low cost" production.

Because delivering universal services frees labor to be priced according to its marginal value added, the "cost" of labor throughout the economy is significantly reduced, especially at the lower skill levels. This in turn, has the knock on effect of reducing the nominal cost of delivering the universal services themselves, because a high proportion of the cost of delivering those services is labor related. In effect, providing universal services reduces the cost of delivering those same services.

A fundamental and progressive effect of universal personal security will be the stimulation and expansion of micro-enterprise. Freed from the pursuit of mere survival, the population will be able to use their more unique skills and interests to create micro-services and products that meet the needs of very small markets. This micro-economy has the ability to boost general satisfaction by allowing specific needs to be met more directly, at the same time that it further enhances the economy by dramatically increasing transaction volumes and efficiency. Child care that allows bicycle repair, that saves resources, that are diverted to power buses, that get people to work faster, that allows more family time. The feedback loops that reinforce the productivity, efficiency and diversity of the economy are endless. Additionally, as more needs are satisfied more directly by micro-suppliers, the dependence on mass production and long-distance transport is lessened, the resilience of local economies is strengthened and production becomes more environmentally sustainable.

Conclusion

When we can separate and distinguish between economic and political policy, we can make effective choices that will lead to the prosperity we desire. We don't need an economic policy that creates jobs, we need a political policy that allows jobs to be created. We don't need economic policies that encumber businesses with social responsibility; we need political policies that deliver real social security.

For our economy we need economic policies, and for our welfare we need political policies; each, unto their own. Far from economic growth resulting in social ills, or social growth resulting in economic ills; economic and social growth are mutually enhancing. Delivering universal social security will not erode productivity, it will enhance it. Unfettered markets will not drive social well-being into the ground, they will lift it up.

If we can just uncouple our unfounded assumptions about the relationship between enterprise and welfare for long enough to see again with clear eyes, based on what we know about ourselves, we can pave a Path to prosperity for all.

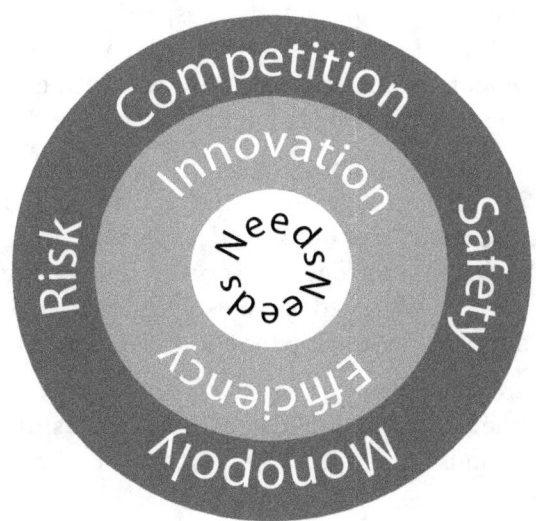

More details can be found at http://www.standardsoflife.com/enterprise

Politicians!

Politics has become a dirty word, and politicians the definition of an untrustworthy profession. It's not hard to see why, from blatant corruption to obvious incompetence the world is littered with good reasons to distrust anyone linked with politics.

Yet everywhere we still yearn for effective action, and nowhere more so than in the political arena. We don't envy anyone the job; either because it is dangerous, or futile, or thankless, or all of those.

Being the chosen representative of your peers in the affairs of state should be an honorable and respectable position, a job that our best and brightest aspire to hold. We need to make being a politician a respected role, if we are to attract the quality leadership that we will need to guide us down The Path.

A politician is a representative of the people, selected to provide executive leadership of the government apparatus and civilian leadership of our societies. This is one of the most important roles that anyone can serve in our society. We not only want, we really need people of character, ability and integrity to provide leadership for our societies in this time.

If we are going to make being a politician a truly meaningful job that garners the best candidates from our constituency, and which commands our respect and trust, what do we expect that job to look like?

Here are some elements of what a political job description should include:

- First and foremost, it has to be a position that allows the holder to get things done, to change what has to be changed and align the priorities of the government with the needs of the people. A politician has to have sufficient power and freedom to make decisions, and hold the civil service responsible for enacting those decisions.

- They need the support of a legal framework that describes the extent and the limits of their authority clearly, so that they can be held responsible for that which they are responsible for, and not for what they're not. A framework that also frees citizens to be responsible for their own actions, as partners in the process.

- We want politicians to be dealmakers, but not consummate dealmakers. We want people who can put a manifesto in front of the electorate, and then go and get it done. Preferably with the support of as many as possible, but where a majority is a mandate.

- They need to be paid well. Well enough to be comfortable, and well enough to make holding the job a reasonable prospect compared to other leadership positions in a constituency. Well enough to want to hold on to the job without other income or taking bribes, but not so well that they can afford to pay bribes!

In summary, a politician should be a leader, with the weight of their popular support behind their executive decision-making, operating in a clear and supporting legal framework, with sufficient pay and administrative support to allow them to focus on being the best representative of their peers that they can be.

Creating that is going to mean changing the political system. These changes are entirely possible in a democracy, and you quite probably live in one. They just require that you, the voter, demand them.

Let's look at some of the attributes of a political system that will attract the kind of candidates that you would be proud to call your representative. Below are some of the facets of such a system, the kind of *super-democracy* discussed earlier in this book and laid out in detail in the Standards of LIFE.

Representative Mandate

In a *super-democracy*, a representative actually has the decision-making power of the voters that support them. A representative who wins 60% of the vote can get things done without the support of another who won 10% of the vote. At the same time, our representatives need to represent us in all our dimensions and diversity. To resolve these two requirements we need an assembly for each constituency in which all voters in a constituency vote for the same slate of candidates, and the elected representatives vote in their assembly with the weight of the share of the vote they received.

For instance, in a state election, everyone in the state votes for the exact same candidates; no subdivisions, no geographic areas and no sub-constituencies. One constituency and one list of candidates that everyone votes from. When all the votes are added up, the candidates with the most votes occupy the available seats in the assembly. But when the assembly votes, each representative votes with the full weight of the number of voters that supported them in the election.

Framework

Politics has to operate within a legal framework where the rule of law is paramount. The law protects the people and describes the limits of the power of the politicians. Part of this framework is a requirement for transparency, which is essential to restraining corruption and keeping the citizenry informed. This is what a constitution is for.

Aspects of a helpful constitution include:

- A legal structure that accords each layer of government with the authority for their particular constituency. Power needs to originate close to the voter in local government, and only be promoted to regional and state layers by choice. This system allows for differences **and** provides harmonization. It uses a legal system called Variable Law,

which allows for the promotion, and retrieval, of aspects of law between layers of government.

- Election to office must be open to all citizens who wish to be candidates, and must provide equal access to mass media for all of them.

- No presidents, no upper chambers or lower houses. Just one assembly for each constituency, full of elected representatives voting with the power of their direct electoral support.

- No term limits: if someone's good at their job and retains the trust of their peers and wants to carry on, they should be able to. (Obviously subject to fair-access election system, see above.)

- No constitutional recognition of political parties. People are free to organize, join and support parties, but individuals are elected irrespective and independent of their party affiliations.

- The assembly needs to be the highest authority in the land, under the Constitution. All civil and military services must report to, and be subservient to, the assembly. All management positions of those services that report directly to the assembly should serve at the will of the assembly, who may appoint replacements as they see fit.

- Public funding of mass media access for campaigning to control the influence of money on elections and politicians.

- No funds from outside the constituency or corporations.

Compensation

- All representatives should be equally compensated and their pay should be proportional to the income of their constituency – something between 5 and 10 times the average income of their constituents would be about right. This links the personal interests of the politician directly to the interest of the majority of their constituents.

- Administrative support and expense should be provided to each representative. It is in everyone's interest that they are well-informed, able to order research and provided sufficient support that allows them to focus on the decisions.

A political system built on these principles, and working within this kind of framework, would be a lot more responsive and responsible to its voters, and would attract candidates who have the desire and ability to effect change.

If we can couple these changes to the job description for a politician with election campaign funding reform, we will lay the foundation for the quality decision making that is so vital to our progress through the difficult times ahead.

Not only can we make politics a clean word again, we must. The changes we need to make to our societies and economies require quality leadership in our democratic systems. We need systemic change, and that means changing our system of representation.

A full description of how *"super-democracy"* is structured can be found at: http://www.StandardsofLIFE.com/Representation.

The full text of the current LIFE Constitutional template can be found at: http://www.StandardsofLIFE.com/Constitutional+Template.

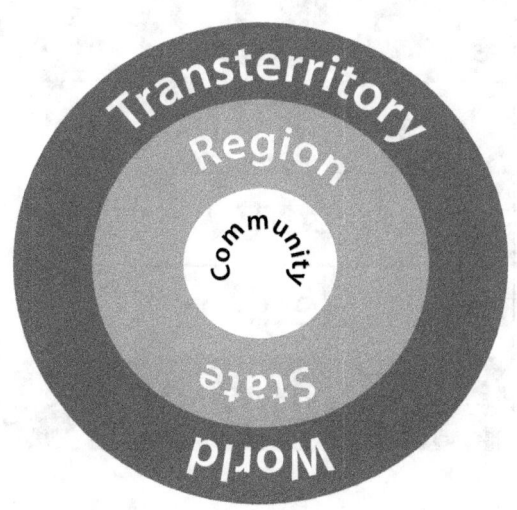

| World |
| Transterritory |
| State |
| Region |
| Community |

Middle East Peace

The touchstone or the tombstone of modern politics, depending on your perspective. Finding a solution to the Israeli-Palestinian conflict, and for peace in the region more generally, has been the avowed intention of many a politician, inside and outside the region, for many a year. But as I write this, the arc of this particular history seems to be bending further and further down.

To quote an editorial leader in one of my favorite political magazines du jour, although quite frankly this could be found in just about any piece written anywhere about the Middle East, "only a negotiated agreement between strong and unified leadership on both sides can provide the security and peace that the Palestinians and Israelis deserve." Really? A top down solution? I guess if either side really had a strong and unified leadership then maybe they would be able to negotiate a peace, but the reality is that neither side does, and they haven't and quite possibly, now they can't. But if we set ourselves up with an insurmountable barrier at the start, how do we expect to make any progress?

The Israeli-Palestinian conflict is an example of a situation that is repeated in many parts of the world, and perhaps that is why it holds such a fascination for so many. The migrations and movements of people are inevitably accompanied by tensions around the matters of political control and resource allocation; this is especially so when they happen in a short period of time, and are accompanied by military might. So finding a solution in the Middle East also provides a guiding light for solutions in many other parts of the world.

Probably the reason that there hasn't been peace in Israel or Palestine is because the obvious solution is not in the interests of any of the parties, except the people that actually live there. There are also many factors that result in external actors having their own interests in the outcome. These distortions have resulted in almost every single state in the entire region having a dysfunctional power structure, and some of those states are also deeply threatened by the obvious solution for Israel-Palestine.

So what is this obvious solution? Democracy. Not 20th century Western-style democracy, the solution here has to be *super-democracy*. *Super-democracy* has a multi-layer structure based on the foundation of Community constituencies. Each Community is fundamentally and constitutionally in complete command of its destiny. Each Community voluntarily associates with other Communities around it to form the larger constituency of a Region, which provides a mechanism for collaboration and sharing. Regions have their own elected governments, and also voluntarily associate with other Regions to form States. All of this is spelled out in a universal constitution adopted by all constituencies.

This solution requires that everyone agrees that peace is the supreme objective. Peace is necessary for our mutual survival, but if we cannot steal ourselves to promote it to the top of our agendas, we cannot have a solution.

The solution to the Israeli-Palestinian conflict is for the people to first divide their land into Communities. Then each Community conducts their own election and forms their own government. Each Community is a voluntary association of residents and must be geographically reasonable (meaning with a population of about 10,000; but not greater than 100,000 or less than 1,000). It can only include land actually inhabited by residents, or land which is closer to a resident than it is to a resident of any other Community. No Community has the right-of-way through any other Community, nor any authority over the people of another Community. All this must happen within the framework of the rule of law so that the use of violence or force is impossible (here is a role in which parties external to the conflict can provide useful assistance as guarantors of the peace, by staffing a "peace force").

This brings us to the first contentious issue: defining who is a resident. This is a key factor in the resolution of these kinds of situations, and must reconcile the desire to make progress immediately, while avoiding the reward of recent aggressions. If a principle is established that recognizes recent displacement, it only encourages displacement in other conflicts. So we pick a date that does not reward recent changes in population placement, and does not seek to redress history. This is known as the Determination Date (D-Date). All those displaced between the D-Date and the current time can claim residency at the place they were on the D-Date. For Israel-Palestine, 1st January 2000 would seem about right, as it reflects the last deadline from the last major peace negotiation, Oslo.

There is a subtlety to this process that we should note explicitly. Those with legal residency of a place as of the D-Date, are those who have the right to select their membership of a specific Community. This does not mean that others currently living there have to move immediately. D-Date residents define the boundaries of each Community, and are automatically citizens of the new Community. As citizens, they are the only voters in the first election for a Community assembly. Once the assembly has been elected, it has authority over the recognition of residency, and the criteria for citizenship. Under the Constitution, residency and citizenship cannot be revoked once established or granted.

Once elected, a Community assembly may grant residency to anyone they wish to, provided they can supply the basic services to them, as is their responsibility under the Constitution. At this point those living within the boundaries of that Community but without residency, will have to move to a Community willing to accept them.

Let's pause for a moment and imagine the state of the process at this point. All the land that is currently defined by the borders of Israel and the Palestinian Territories is operating as a suspended state with a caretaker administration. That administration is charged solely with the maintenance of vital infrastructure and social services, with the aim of minimizing the disruption of people's ordinary lives. Over the caretaker administration there is a "peace force", consisting of Israeli, Palestinian and international forces charged with the enforcement of law and order, and the prevention of violence. So the people are effectively living in a suspended political environment that will last until such time as Community, Region and State elections have been held. This period of suspension should be less than two years.

As Community boundaries are defined, those Communities proceed immediately to the election of their assembly. As soon as the Community governments have been elected they can assume control of policy within their boundaries. One of the first matters that the assembly has to attend to is the business of establishing their Regional affiliation, bearing in mind that they must be geographically contiguous with any Region they wish to be a part of. Each Community can start making decisions about what aspects of law they wish to retain unto themselves, and what they want to promote to higher layers; as well as establishing a court system and local police force tasked with the maintenance of basic law and order inside that Community.

Within a few months it should be possible to draw the boundaries of Regions based on the self-determined, voluntary associations of the Communities. Once Regional boundaries are established, there can be Regional elections to form Regional governments. At this point the Communities and their Regions can begin the important work of building their infrastructures, and assuming responsibility from the caretaker government for the provision of core services to their constituents. Much work can be done on formalizing the Variable Law structure so that, by the time that state elections are scheduled, each Region has clarity about those aspects of law that have been promoted to them by their Communities, and therefore which aspects they have the option of promoting to their State. This is important because what the States will have authority for will be critical in shaping the manifestos of candidates for the State assemblies.

At this juncture, the Communities will be in control of their own environment; including the definition of their migration policies, and responsible to their constituents for the safety and functionality of their Community. The Communities have made their initial selection of Regional association, although they are at liberty to change that association at their own election. As each constituency elects its own government, and assumes control of its specific area, the role of the "peace force" will be diminished. It becomes solely the guarantor of peace between Regions, until such time as State elections have been held.

This devolution of power and control down to the individual Communities will greatly empower the large majority of the population that seeks peace and sustainable prosperity. Admittedly, there is likely to be a concentration of those people that would seek to impose their worldview on others into certain Communities of like mind; however they will be dependent on the cooperation of surrounding Communities, and this is likely to influence their positions over time. This process does not force any Community to change its mind or take up any particular position, so those who wish to maintain extremist or isolationist attitudes will be free to do so, within the constraints of the rule of law and the Constitution.

Eventually there will be State elections. Each State will cover an area defined by those Regions which choose to associate into that State; this may be a single state, it may be two states or it may even be multiple states. By this stage in the process, the Communities and Regions will have determined for themselves those aspects of power and control that they wish to retain unto themselves, so the eventual governments of whatever States are formed will have a much narrower remit than we see in the typical nationstate of today.

At the end of this process of building up layers of enfranchisement, starting at Communities which self assemble into Regions, and then Regions which form States, there will be democratic institutions in place which can assume the full range of governmental responsibilities from the caretaker

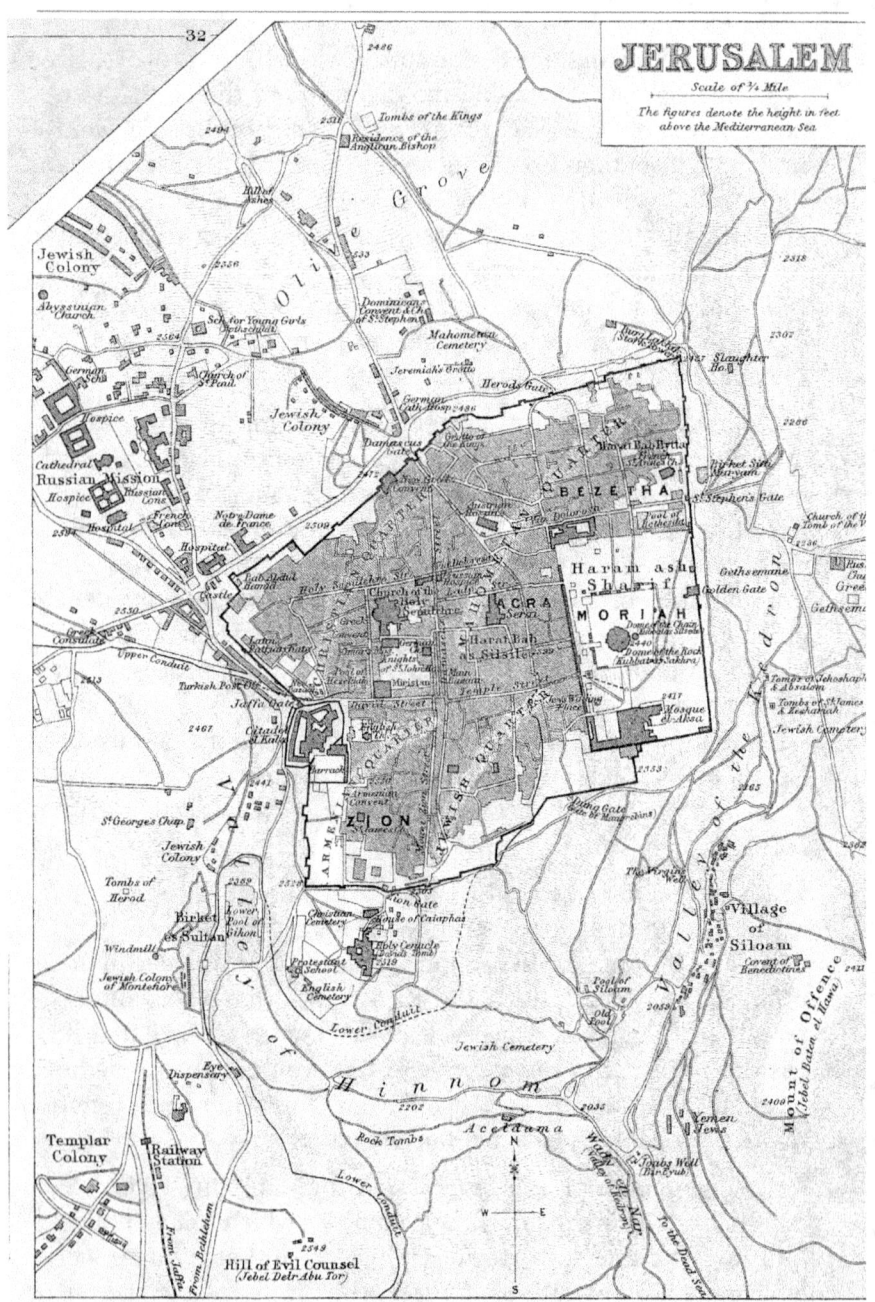

Map of Jerusalem, 1921

administration. The final map will not be drawn until after the final State election. Even then the map will remain fluid, as Communities and Regions retain the right to change their associations at the behest of their citizens.

The next logical step would be for the States to form a Transterritory with other States in the region; however this will require that those other nations go through the same enfranchisement process that the peoples of the former Israel-Palestine will have completed.

It's not a particularly bold solution, nor is democracy a new idea. What it is, is the determined application of a system that is inherently natural and just – that is the hallmark of The Path. The two greatest challenges are likely to be restraining the violent tendencies of those who would rather not be subject to the rigors of democracy, and restricting the interference of external actors of every hue, from every corner of the world. The solutions to problems in an area must be developed by the people living in that area. This is a plain, obvious and unavoidable fact. Those outside the area must accept the consequences of true democracy.

Does this solution require that Israel and Palestine have "strong and unified leadership" today, before they embark on this process? I don't think so. Only to the extent that it is necessary to make the decision to start down The Path. One of the beauties of the *super-democratic* path is that it removes the need for small elites to negotiate extremely complex and intricate resolutions to the many and specific problems on the ground. It does this by devolving those responsibilities down to the individual communities most affected. They are the ones most able to arbitrate the minutia contextualized in the benefits of the peace that they seek most urgently, and will feel most keenly.

The basic question that is resolved through this process is: "Does this piece of land belong to that country or this country?" It's really a nonsensical question because, of course, the answer is: it belongs to the people that live there, and it's up to them to decide what country they want to be part of. All that the *super-democratic* process does, is provide a mechanism that allows people to determine their own future, their own identity and to make their own associations.

There are those who call this solution naïve. They point out that on the extremes of both Israeli and Palestinian opinion there are those for whom peace is not the ultimate objective. They are right. The question is whether we wish to be held hostage by the shortsighted. There must be a solution that leads to the cessation of hostilities and provides the opportunity for all to focus on the future, because we are all mutually dependent on reaching that destination. What this solution does is emphasize the dignity of self-determination, and in so doing provides a path out of the quagmire. It does not pretend that today's reality is anything other than what it is and it does not describe a way forward that will not have difficulties, challenges and complications. But this is a realistic framework that builds on the humanity of individuals in their communities to create a structure that allows differences to live next to each other. For surely, a way forward must be found and it must be found now. Inaction and despair are not solutions. There are children in every corner of the land who will thank their forebears for persevering through the clouded landscape to bring peace to their lives today.

On a wider note, it is almost inconceivable to believe that the enfranchisement of Israeli and Palestinian communities to determine their own futures will not have ramifications for surrounding states, and perhaps the entire world. Those who are interested in navigating The Path to a sustainable future must be ready and willing to help those states, their governments and their people, make an orderly transition to *super-democracy* themselves.

Everybody everywhere in the world should live in a *super-democratic* system, and if we're serious about reaching the destination of a sustainably prosperous future, we need to set about making this a reality where we live... now!

A full description of how "super democracy" is structured can be found at:
http://www.StandardsofLIFE.com/Representation.

The Digital Kimono

One of the most shocking developments today is the proliferation of digital surveillance and identity profiling, with little or scant regard for the protection of individual liberties or the sanctity of our society as a whole. What makes this particularly galling, is that despite there being so much well-respected, high quality and widely read literature on the subject, both our governments, and we as citizens, have failed miserably to contain or manage the risks associated with the digital theft of our real freedom.

The greatest tragedy of this abuse of our digital identities is that it erodes our confidence in the very technologies that we need to forge our Path to prosperity. We need digital communications technology to drive the blossoming of micro-economic activity, the *super-economy* of our future. But this is only going to happen if the average citizen can trust the technology to be their asset, rather than an instrument of those that might oppress or manipulate them.

The status we have now is rather like wearing a kimono. If we really wanted to maintain our privacy we would have to abstain from virtually every aspect of modern life: no credit cards, no e-mail, no telephone, no taxes, not attending any major event or walking the streets of any town or city. But we don't live that way, and who would want to live under those conditions? The trouble is that we assume that there is a rule of law in the digital world, just as there is in the real world. In actuality the digital world has streaked ahead of our legal protections, and operates in a space with about as much oversight and regulation as the credit default swap and derivatives markets, i.e. none at all. If you open your kimono even a crack, you may as well be naked. In the digital world there is nothing to prevent a whole host of people and organizations from tracking your every move, snooping on your communications, storing private information about you, and correlating that with who knows what they think they know about your friends. To make matters even worse, they're going to mix your identity up with the data they have about everyone else in the world with a name spelled vaguely similarly to yours, and whomever now has your old cell phone numbers.

Neither politicians nor the senior members of our legal establishment have had the technical understanding to be able to grasp the fibers of the digital world. We need to subject digital information to the same rigors and standards that we have developed in the pursuit of, and protection for, the liberty of the average citizen – liberties won at great personal cost to many over the centuries. The digital world needs the rule of law, just as much as the real world does.

We must start by accepting that digital identity is part of our present and our future. Once we've done that, we can move on to purposefully create a secure digital identity system that has our privacy and the protection of our freedom at its core. It's not too late, but we really need to get on top of this one right now.

We need a founding legal framework that enshrines our right to privacy, and includes the right to review any personal information held by any other party. Once we have codified the concept of digital privacy and enshrined the rights of the individual to that, we can move on to use technology in ways that will truly serve us.

A secure digital identity system is possible, and we already have all the technology necessary to build one. The security of the system and the protection of our freedom are not to be found in the technology itself, but in how it is structured and deployed. By separating identity from information, we can control our exposure and simplify the system. Imagine if your medical records at your doctor's offices did not have your name on them; they have all the information about your health, but only a key to your identity. That key only links the information to you when you turn the key in the lock, using parts of your private identity. That is how digital identity should work.

Here are some of the vital elements of a functional digital identity system, to give you an idea of what we are going to have to build in order to harness the benefits of modern technology to serve us all, as we travel down the Path.

- One of the most important standards, is to avoid the collection of large amounts of data in one place. Data should be dispersed, as much as possible, into separated storage silos, each with their own security and access controls. This limits the exposure of any security breach, and makes it almost impossible to mine for information without the appropriate permissions.

- A functional digital identity system will also allow the individual to disclose only those parts of their identity that they wish to, for any given transaction. Buying a train ticket and cashing a check can require completely different levels of identity verification.

- All this can be done without obliging anyone to carry any form of digital identity card, certificate or token. It can all be achieved with a combination of biometric and biognostic information. If we value our freedom, we can never let it be an offense to be peaceful in public without a form of identity.

- Another important feature of a secure system is that it requires the buildout of a secure network that is used to transmit sensitive information, separate from the general access Internet.

Interoperability between the distributed systems is required for the overall functionality of the system, and that means that we need universal standards for the basic elements of digital identity. Without such standards, the systems and the data they contain will remain veiled behind the barriers of commercial intellectual property.

The xID standards developed as part of the Standards of LIFE provide a framework for the key elements we need, including:

- The content of a digital ID record
- A mechanism for verifying the quality of an identity match
- Security
- Audit, search, investigation and management processes

We need to start building a secure, privacy-orientated, public, global digital identity system now. The timescale to implement this is a minimum of three years, and is more likely to be five years, which is half the time we have available to turn our societies into functioning *super-trio* environments.

We can, and must, start building different aspects of The Path now, and implementing a digital identity system is a keystone element that will make full *super-trio* functionality both easier and faster.

The reason why all of this matters, is because we need to be able to trust digital systems. Digital communications are vital to enabling the new micro-economy, essential for an energy-efficient future and necessary for administrating our new *super-democracies*. So we need to reach a place where we can be reasonably assured that allowing our identities to be digitized is not sacrificing our freedom. We need underwear under our kimonos.

For more details about how to create a secure digital identity system go to:
http://www.standardsoflife.com/xID

~~~ Musical Interlude ~~~

The Indian Highway Problem

I was sitting in the waiting room of a garage the other day with my son, while I scribbled notes for this book. I reached the end of a section and, looking for inspiration, I turned to him and asked him what problem in the world he thought we should think about next.

"The Indian highways." was his response.

We had just returned from a three week tour around India and obviously the many hours we spent dodging death as we traveled the roads, at one end of the country to the other, had left an impression on him.

At first I simply threw up my hands and said that I didn't think that was truly a solvable problem. Then I remembered that there isn't a problem we've created that we can't also have a solution for.

During our vacation we had traveled by car along a section of India's new "National Highway" and encountered the normal array of miscellaneous traffic from pedestrians, to ox carts, to huge over laden Tata trucks. But what made this particularly incongruous was that this was a toll road, and for at least a mile either side of the tollbooths there were fences to prevent the entrance of non-vehicular traffic. In remembering this, it struck me that if you build a highway through an area that has no paved local roads, this was bound to happen; people will find a way onto the highway. So the answer is that you have to build local roads for local traffic, first.

"Local roads first."

An interesting analogy for building The Path to a Future, eh?

LOVE Thy Neighbor

If we are to make the urgent progress that we need to on The Path to a Future, we need to do it together. Areas of blight and conflict will be a drag on all of our progress, because they will suck resources away from more effective uses. The people in conflict are unlikely to participate in the global initiatives needed, such as tackling climate change. We need a coherent policy structure that protects the progress of those that are already building The Path, and provides on-ramps to The Path for the victims of oppression and conflict today, but who will join us tomorrow.

One of the more curious spectacles of our time is the apparent futility, cluelessness and impotence of the world's governments, especially of the richest countries, in developing coherent strategies toward so-called "rogue states" or "failed states". What we mean by a "rogue state" is that their leadership is unresponsive to the plight of their population, at the same time that they reject pleas from other countries to join the community of nations. They fail to treat their people with respect, and refuse to submit to the principles of democracy. What we mean by "failed states" are places where there is no established order because the interests of external actors trump and exclude the interests of the populations that live there.

As always, we must start with a clear picture of what is. What is happening in these disrupted states is that one hand is supporting them, while the other points at them accusingly. This happens because the foreign policy of most nations refers only to their diplomatic relationship; it does not include their commercial or military relationships. No rogue state has the capacity to stand alone; so we have to ask how it is that their leadership continues in power. Someone, somewhere, is supporting them.

When the Americans announced an embargo on the supply of luxury goods to North Korea in 2007, did you wonder to yourself how on earth luxury goods were getting there before the embargo? When the Zimbabwean army doesn't run out of bullets or gasoline, do you ask yourself why? The answer is fairly obvious. Somebody is trading with the regimes of these states. It turns out that quite often those traders and corporations are based in the very same nations as the governments that are publicly denouncing the actions and intransigence of the regimes. Not to put too fine a point on it, we are hypocrites. This is not lost on people around the world and corrupts the validity of all inter-national policy.

If we, the people, are to honestly represent our intentions and belief in the importance and ascendancy of democracy, the rule of law and human rights, then we have to have the courage to include all aspects of our society's interactions in our foreign policies. We don't need to be shy about our desire to see regime change in other states, because if they're not engaged on The Path to sustainable prosperity, then they're part of the problem. But desiring regime change is not the same as imposing regime change. The primary objective of the policies we should have towards others is to ensure that we are not supporting governments that are not engaged in the solutions.

Let's examine a counter claim, often made, that the separation of commercial and diplomatic spheres serves the populations of both countries. I guess it could be called "trickle up democracy", because it says that creating a wealthier populace will lead them to demand democracy and their rights, and that commercial engagement facilitates this process. The logic of this argument rests on an oversimplification of the relationships we have with other nations and flies in the face of observable facts. Of course there are countries with which we have rich and complex trading relationships that obviously benefit the people on both sides, but doing business with rogue states quite obviously does not benefit their people. Another claim is that the destabilizing impact of the collapse of a rogue state's government on its neighbours is reason to support the rogue. This need not be the case, if we have a coherent plan to support the population's transition to a functioning *super-trio* state after the collapse of their oppressors.

What we can do, is to ensure that any trade with states is contributing to the forward progress of all. Where states are not investing in the freedom, security and prosperity of their people, we can do it for them. We can withhold taxes and duties on their behalf, and keep those funds ready for use whenever it becomes possible to make the investments.

We can develop a simple scale for how we will work with our neighbors, depending on their adherence to universal rights and representation; a scale of the extent to which we will engage with and support other countries and their establishments. A set of policies that provides assistance to the populations of suppressive states when we can, but which prevents empowering of their rulers when we can't.

It so happens that the acronym for this relationship scale is easy to remember: LOVE. (This means we can truly have a foreign policy based on the phrase "love thy neighbour"!) By using LOVE we will have a consistent approach to how we relate to others, and they will be able to clearly understand where they stand with us.

The L in LOVE stands for "Life affirming". This is the category for relationships we have with other countries that observe the same *super-trio* of peace, security and sustainable prosperity that we will. In these cases we can be confident that the relationship does not require close regulation because both parties are operating by the same standards, and the populations have the ability to protect their own interests through their democracies. L countries cooperate on joint interests and all have foreign policies based on LOVE.

The O in LOVE stands for "Oppressive". This refers to states that have not adopted the *super-trio* that L states have. In these cases trade can be open, but must be regulated to ensure a level playing field and to prevent contortion of the LOVE policy standards. If they don't provide *super-security* services for their people, we collect the equivalent costs for them by taxing their exports as well as the profits of companies operating in the O state but based in our country. Then we return the revenues to non-governmental organizations in those countries that are providing the missing *super-security* services. If they are not collecting carbon taxes, will collect their carbon taxes for them. Trading with O states would include the monitoring of the origin content of products from O, so that any sub-content from V or E states can be treated according to the standards below.

V states are those that use "Violence" to suppress their populations. They might be imprisoning people without due process, violently suppressing freedom of speech or allowing the use of violence by one community against another inside their country. The primary policy concern here is to distinguish between the rulers and the people. We all know that people everywhere want the same things: freedom, respect and dignity. So we want to support the people, and not be enablers of their suppression. Trade with V countries should be closely governed, and exclude all financial services, luxury goods and potential military- or police-use products. Remaining trade would be subject to duties designed to collect funds for the implementation of *super-democracy* in the V country. The costs of implementing a democratic process would be estimated, and applied to all goods and services traded. The duties would be collected in a reserve fund that will be released to the people of the country when they can implement a *super-democratic* system. No rights or services would be afforded to the ruling elite that they do not allow for all of their own people, e.g. travel.

In cases where there has been an "Extreme" breakdown in the social fabric, what are called "failed states", all trade is restricted and only direct support to the people is allowed. These are E states.

The LOVE policy stances apply to all people and businesses uniformly. For instance Zimbabwe would be classified as a V country, and so all businesses with Zimbabwean interests based in our nation would be subject to the duties and restrictions applicable to that category, and any profits derived from trade with Zimbabwe subject to the appropriate withholdings. Or in the case of petroleum/gas exports from Burma, the companies facilitating the construction of the petro-infrastructure as well as the products manufactured in countries that consume the energy exports, would be subject to withholding taxes on behalf of the people of Burma.

One of the great things about the LOVE thy neighbor framework for external relations is that it can be used universally by all *super-trio* communities, regions and states – even to relationships between themselves. The compensatory duties levied can be pooled and the value of those funds advertised directly to the people of the affected countries, so that they know what level of support is available to them, once they change their regimes and start down The Path with us.

It will not be perfect, it will be hard to assess appropriate withholdings and it is inevitably subjective, but it is a comprehensive framework with clear principles that can be activated and administered easily.

We need clear guidelines by which our politicians, businessmen and the military can operate, and LOVE provides them with a brightly lit playing field.

More details about LOVE can be found at:
http://www.standardsoflife.com/external+relations

The Mind of Production

To support *super-democracy*, *super-security* and build a thriving *super-economy* we to need to make substantial investments in our societies. To make those changes to our infrastructure we will have to leverage the strengths of private enterprise to help us reach our public policy objectives.

We struggle with the interface between public initiatives and private enterprise, and the debate tends to be rather crudely proposed as pitting right intention against effective action, as if they were incompatible. In fact they are mutually complimentary, and both absolutely necessary if we are to reach our goals.

We need to mix the public good with the effectiveness of the market. We need to manage strategically important assets like energy and housing, and avoid the perils of mismanagement and misdirection that so easily infiltrate incentive-weak endeavors. There is a beneficial role for public-private partnerships to partake in the management of strategic resources, so long as a clearly identified structure is followed.

The easy part is acknowledging that all sides have valid contributions to make (see the chapter *Economics 001* earlier in this section). Easy, but important. There is a place for the public interest, for entrepreneurial zeal, for the efficiency of the market and for the efforts of motivated workers – all these are necessary ingredients to forge the Path to our future.

The challenge is balancing the efficacy of our efforts with the efficiencies of our processes. This is where it really helps to have a firm grasp on our objectives, and clear sight of the principles. We will not get to where we want to go if we don't leverage our talents, and we cannot tell where we will end up if we don't decide where we are going. We need to set clear objectives, and achieve them with as much natural efficiency as we can muster.

When we look at the buildout of *super-security* we can see that there is much work to be done in each area. Houses need to be built and maintained, food harvested and prepared, digital communications networks laid and connected. All of these efforts will require effective public-private partnerships. The public initiative and intention to make them happen, and the private effort and ingenuity to get them done as efficiently and effectively as possible. This means we need to understand the interface between public institutions and private enterprises, and establish ground rules for their partnerships that will deliver the results we all need.

Quite often, a brief introduction to the concept of *super-security* leads people to immediately assume that it must mean the public ownership of the means of production. This is not true. In fact history has shown, time and again, that incentive is the grease that allows the wheel of production to turn effectively. It is the mind of production that we seek to bio-mimic; left and right sides operating inside a single skull, balanced to achieve the desired objective. The private/left brain helps make the intentions of the public/right brain become reality.

The function of public policy is to determine the objective, the destination and the end result desired. In the case of *super-security* that means defining the exact nature of the services available, in terms of both cost and content. To reach the desired destination, public policy must engage the private sector to implement the services whenever possible, practical and appropriate.

In engaging with the private sector it is important that the public sector focus on three things:

- clearly specified objectives
- transparency of process
- open competition between private suppliers

If the public policy cannot provide all three of these, then engaging with the private sector is likely to fail and will be subject to corruption. In these cases the endeavour must be a wholly public effort.

Assuming the public policy is clear, transparent and open, there are three attributes of private sector participation necessary for success:

- adherence to the objective's clearly stated quality and content standards
- responsibility for meeting the standards (i.e. risk)
- reward for taking the responsibility

Private enterprise is reliant on an incentive for effective participation, and the orientation of their risk and reward around specified objectives is necessary for their successful involvement.

This risk-reward balance necessarily includes the possibility of failure (the ultimate risk), and the inclusion of private enterprise in the fulfilling of a public objective requires the open disclosure of what will happen in the event of failure. Failure will result in costs, and even if most of those costs fall to the private partner, the public side will inevitably shoulder some of the impact, even if it is only in the form of delay. Private entities and the public must understand that the risk of additional cost exists, and the reason that those risks are acceptable is because the benefits of the partnership exceed the risks.

There are seven elements to a public initiative:

- specification
- design
- construction
- maintenance
- operation
- management
- ownership

The beginning and the end are quintessentially in the public domain; the steps in the middle of the process are where private partners add the value necessary for success.

The objective is defined by the public policy. The specification of the attributes, standards and quality of the objective are substantially a public responsibility, although it is beneficial to seek input and ideas from the private sector as part of the specification process.

The design of the product or service can be developed by private parties and selected by public representatives.

The private sector can, and should, build as well as maintain – those two go together, so that the responsibility for remediating defects in the construction belong to the manufacturer.

The operation of the initiative can be provided as a service by private contractors who may also assist with the management of the output, although ultimate management responsibility rests with the public entities.

Finally, ownership of the output of any public initiative belongs to the public.

By following this clear path for public-private partnerships, we can deliver the best possible results while protecting the public investment and leveraging the market. The two partners can and do work well together, when the roles and responsibilities are clearly demarcated.

So let's see how this works in the real world by using a couple of examples raised earlier: housing and food.

The public objective is secure shelter for those in need.

- The public authority draws up a specification that includes both facilities minimums and cost maximums.

- Builders and designers submit designs for approval.

- Once a design is selected, the contract to build and maintain the housing units is put out to bid, with the winner having responsibility for construction and 20 years of maintenance.

- A public management office issues a request for bids for the operation of the housing, perhaps a one-year contract with four annual options to renew.
- The housing is owned by the public.

The public objective is nutritious sustenance, and is expressed as a specification for content and prohibited ingredients.

- Private companies submit bids for designs that meet the specification and manufacturers receive approval for their products.
- Consumers choose the products they want from the approved manufacturers and pay the market price for their product.
- The public objective is achieved, the consumer has a degree of choice that allows them to manage their diet and producers participate competitively.

In each case the producers are not public employees, and have the opportunity to reap rewards for quality products in a competitive market. It's a win-win situation, and demonstrates that delivering *super-security* to our populations does not mean a state-controlled economy or a communist system.

Combining the devolution of power down to local communities, with the development of the micro-*super-economy*, we will enable diverse and mutually rewarding public-private partnerships on The Path to a sustainably prosperous future.

Flat Sharing

For my entire working life the conventional wisdom seems to have been that only a mug would pay their full share of taxes, and that it was every citizen's duty to reduce their responsibilities in this area to a minimum. Those who succeeded in paying the least amount of taxes have generally been lauded as heroes. It's a shame really, and it has never been my perspective on the matter. I have concluded that it is just another sign of the disconnect between people and their government that leads them to such a cavalier attitude to their relationship with the society that they live in and depend on.

To give you an example of how twisted this logic has become, the managers of the pension funds (into which we are all paying in the hopes of providing for our future security) are encouraging the businesses that they invest in to reduce their taxes as much as possible, so that they can feed more profits into the pension funds. So the people in charge of the money that is supposed to provide for our old age, are motivated to reduce our other forms of social security as much as possible. Each little part of it may make sense to the people involved, but the big picture doesn't make sense at all.

To move forward on The Path to a Future we need to have a different relationship with the people that live around us and our society as a whole, such that we voluntarily pay our taxes and consider it an extremely good deal!

There are two primary reasons why people object to paying their taxes. First, they don't see a relationship between their contribution to the state and their circumstances. Second, they believe that the system is fundamentally corrupt, with uneven collection and wasteful distribution.

Given that we know that our sustainably prosperous future requires the co-development of *super-security* and a *super-economy*, this problem relationship with taxation is something that we have got to resolve. We've got to reach a place where we are voluntarily paying taxes because we understand what a difference our contribution makes to our own lives, we can see that it is being collected fairly, and we know that it is being spent appropriately.

Now you might consider that making all of that a reality to be a pretty tall order, but I hope to show you that a few simple changes will make it a short order.

The first thing to do is to separate income taxes from all the other kinds of taxes, and then we'll come back to things like sales and property taxes after we have dealt with income tax. Income taxes have the broadest reach, collect the most revenue, and are the least subject to the exercise of choice, and for these reasons they require special treatment.

In a *super-trio* society there is a direct linkage between income taxes and *super-security* that makes it easy to understand why you're paying them and what the money is being used for. In a *super-trio* society income taxes are used only to pay for *super-security* services. This means that the money is spent in a way that everybody can agree is essential and important. Furthermore, by linking the amount of money raised from income taxes to the cost of providing *super-security* services, there is a direct connection that everyone can see and understand.

The next thing we need to do is to simplify what we mean by "income": everything that anyone receives in a form or manner that can be spent, is counted as income. It doesn't matter if the money came as wages from a job, lottery winnings, the sale of an appreciated asset or an inheritance, it all counts as income. If you get it, and you didn't have it before, and you can spend it: it's income.

Great, that's two really important bits under our belt: what counts as income, and what we spend income taxes on. Only a short way to go!

The final step is to create the relationship between the amount of taxes that need to be raised, and the amount of income available to raise it from; this gives you your basic rate of income tax, say 30%. You could simply leave it at that, the traditional "flat tax", or you can modify it with a progressive tax regime linked to the median earnings of a taxpayer, which I think is a vastly superior system. With a progressive tax linked to median earnings, you can build in universal incentives to raise average earnings at the same time as containing *super-security* costs. When the basic rate of income tax is linked to median earnings it creates an incentive for everyone to keep the costs of universal services low, because those costs determine the basic tax rate. The linkage also makes it in the best interests of the highest earners to raise the median earnings of the whole population, because that reduces their personal tax burden.

Frankly, the manner in which tax rates are distributed across income ranges can be something that varies from constituency to constituency, and is the subject of internal political policy. The point is that with three simple changes we have dramatically changed the face of income taxation; we have made it understandable, relevant and fair. By clearly establishing what income taxes can be used for, we have created a direct link between the quality of the life we lead and the quantity of taxes we pay.

And these are all changes that any government worth its name could implement within months. They simplify the tax code and shift the political burden from deciding how much to charge people for the right to be a citizen, to how much should be spent to provide the security that is the right of every citizen.

It is important to note here that there is a reasonable maximum rate of income tax, beyond which incentive is eroded, and the legitimacy of its claim to be a voluntary contribution is degraded. That reasonable maximum is a rate of 50%. If someone cannot keep at least half of what they have earned, then the social contract has become distinctly suspect. Given this maximum rate for income tax, there is an automatic and appropriate ceiling on the budget available for *super-security* services.

A quick perusal of the contents of *super-security* services might leave you wondering how we're going to pay for the military, subsidies to various industries, park maintenance or any of the other myriad of expenses currently included in many government budgets, and which are not part of the seven basic *super-security* services. You're right, none of these is included in the specifications for *super-security*, and therefore they cannot be paid for with income taxes. This has the advantage of making income taxes universally acceptable, and the second advantage of shifting the burden for all other government expenditures on to sales taxes, property taxes and taxes on corporate profits. I'm sure that these matters will be the subject of much debate, and may well result in an elevated interest in the political dialogues of our communities – so be it!

This leaves us with the other three primary categories of taxation, aside from income taxes: property taxes, sales taxes and taxes on the profits earned by businesses.

Property taxes are relatively easy to deal with, because property always has a location. So it makes sense that any taxes levied on property are collected and spent as locally to that property as is possible. Effectively, this means that they are collected at the Community level, and spent there too.

Sales taxes come in two different forms: taxes simply designed as a way to raise revenues, and taxes applied to products as part of an effort to maintain the quality of market mechanisms. In the case of the latter, for instance carbon taxes, the appropriate level is determined based on analysis of what is necessary to balance any distortions in normal functioning of the market and, while this is bound to be the subject of political policy, its primary intention is correctional and the revenues specifically directed to the maintenance of that market. Common sales taxes, applied to anything except *super-security* services, are a flexible and convenient way to raise revenues that can be appropriated for whatever purpose is desired. Sales taxes can and should be defined by each layer of government, as suits the needs of that layer.

The level of taxation levied on the profits of businesses is entirely subject to the political aspirations of the society within which those businesses operate. Having provided for the basic needs and security of the citizenry using funds raised from income taxes, you could argue that there is no reason to have corporate taxes. In reality it is quite likely that the society will aspire to various ambitions over and above the provision of *super-security* services, and to the extent that they are unwilling to fund those ambitions out of property or sales taxes, then corporate taxes are a likely candidate.

As well as proper representation, a fair and comprehensible tax system is vital for our transformation, and we can have such a system within months. Its implementation will be transformative for the role of government, the equity of our societies and our ability to focus on building our future. This is a step we can take, we must take, and which will be the equivalent of changing gears in our progression.

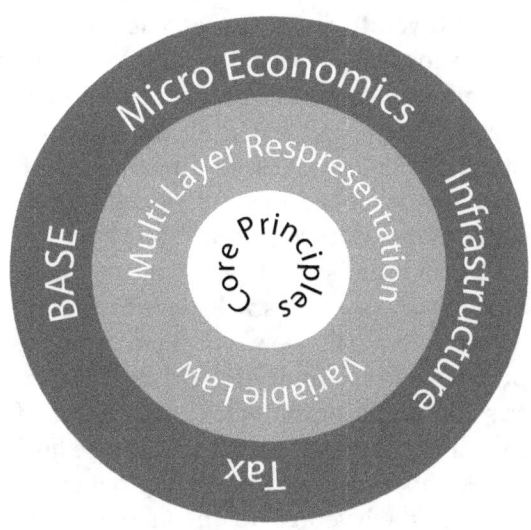

More details about this tax structure can be found at:
http://www.standardsoflife.com/taxes

Dear Retiree

A message from your friendly taxpayer:

We, the taxpayers, are writing to you on the occasion of your upcoming, or passed, retirement age with important information about the benefits and services that will be available to you in the future.

The mirage of perpetually self-sustaining industrial economic growth is beginning to break up before our eyes. It didn't last long. Born in the 1930s and 40s, it was apparent by the 1980s that a Social Security benefit system that promised cash pensions and leisure in later years to every citizen, was dependent on unsustainable rates of economic growth. We are living longer, expenses have increased and we can no longer keep up with the costs.

We recognize that promises, made on the back of unrealistic calculations about growth, longevity and cost, may have incentivized you to forgo the satisfaction of a quality life then, in return for the promise of comfortable leisure later. This incentive became so vital to the growth of wealth, that to actually call it the sham that it always was was not in the interests of the ownership classes who had most of the wealth at the time. When it looked like the gig was up in the 1980s, approximately half way through your working life, the story was re-spun into a promise that everyone who made it into the private ownership class would still be able to attain the promise of leisurely retirement. This new retirement promise was based on your private pension and your private property, but the promise was still based on unrealistic projections for growth. Whenever the hint of recession appeared on the horizon during recent decades, those in charge at the top pulled every trick in the book to notch the leverage up one more click, in the hopes of sustaining the mirage just a little longer.

Now we know. Now we know that the math was always flawed. We know that stock markets go down as far as they go up. We know that having debts greater than one third of your lifetime's output is unsustainable, and therefore there's only so much property values can increase before they become unaffordable. And so falls the final curtain hiding the organ player, and reveals the mirage for what it always was – an illusion.

There is a sustainable model for our retirement. Ironically, a much more fulfilling and satisfying model, but it doesn't provide for great disparities of wealth. In this sustainable model you don't sacrifice your working life for a retired life; instead you live a rich and fulfilling life all the time. A sustainable standard of life, albeit at a lower standard of living. Instead of "working our hearts out", we will live with our hearts; instead of "dying to succeed", we will succeed in our lives.

What we can afford to promise each other is the basic necessities for a full and productive life. Shelter, sustenance, healthcare, education and access to information and transport, with legal protection for our dignity. That's the new pension plan. A place to live in; quality food sufficient to sustain your health; primary and preventative health care; lifelong educational opportunities; abundant access to information; transportation around your community and a legal system that protects your rights in conjunction with everyone else's rights. All this is yours; guaranteed, realistic and affordable, plus whatever else you can add to it.

It may be that we will be able to afford to pay you a pension, especially if you have become incapacitated from productive work, but we must take care of our responsibilities for the basics first. We must ensure that everyone has shelter and food and all the other services, accessible in equal measure to those in need. We're sure you can understand that.

Those of you disappointed that you didn't live in those few decades when the mirage looked oh so real, we empathize. Your disappointment and frustration are very real, and we share them. The task now must be to implement what we can afford, to replace the illusion with reality, and to do so as quickly as possible.

On the bright side, life will be much more fun and people will have more time to take care of each other. It will be safer and richer, in the human sense of the word.

We will convert your cash benefits into universal services. It's not hard to do, but it will involve a transition. We must ready the services before we can stop the benefits payments, and that means we must move rapidly to deploy the services. There will be an investment period while we make the transition, but we can do it in less than three years. So in three years time, you will stop getting the same pension check from us every month, and instead you will get everything you were going to spend that check on.

We'd like to ask for your support as we make these changes, but that would be disingenuous, as we don't have any choice. We can't do anything else, we don't have the money. [Your support would still be appreciated.]

We will be erecting a "Wall of Disgrace" in your neighborhood, and we invite you to donate your rotten food items to the wall armory. The wall will be decorated with the pictures of all the politicians and others who fabricated and perpetuated the myth of "self-sustaining growth" and we invite you to come by, any time, and express your feelings. A friendly, volunteer taxpayer will provide you with materials from the wall armory, that you can use to make an offering to your least favorite mirage maker's image. (All used materials will be collected and composted, should you wish to add some to your garden later.)

Thank you for taking the time to read this message and we sincerely thank you for all the years of hard work you put into paying for your elders' retirements. In appreciation, we look forward to providing you with the best services we can afford and to spending time with you hearing about your lifetimes, and absorbing the wisdom you have gained.

Yours sincerely,

The Future Generations

For Rent: One Planet

We have a resource crunch on our hands and we need to figure out what to do about it, now!

There are certain variables that are outside of our control. Notably, the quantity of planet and atmosphere are distinctly fixed. The variables that are within our control are fairly simple:

One planet available, includes one planet's worth of energy, one atmosphere, plenty of weather, good views. Requires gardening. Lease length subject to negotiation with landlady.

- how many of us there are on the planet
- how much we consume
- how much we waste

The math that got us to where we are now isn't very complicated either. We live on a planet whose climate cycles between warmer and cooler periods based on certain tolerances for the absorption, retention and reflection of the energy it receives from its sun. Our planet has a natural capacity to absorb and recycle a certain amount of the gases in its atmosphere as part of its natural cycle. For the last 150 years the number of humans inhabiting the planet, the amount of energy we consume and the amount of waste that we emit has grown dramatically. During this time we have exceeded our planet's natural ability to absorb and recycle our waste gases, and that, in turn, has pushed our planet's cyclical tolerance limits beyond anything since our appearance here.

The result of changing the balance of gases in our atmosphere is unpredictable in detail, but seems quite likely to dramatically change weather patterns in general. The tolerances within which humans inhabit the planet are a minute subset of the planet's tolerances for climactic change, so it is unrealistic to expect our planet to rebalance its atmosphere within a timescale aligned to our survival. Therefore it is incumbent on us to make the changes necessary to limit the unbalancing, and then leverage our planet's natural capacity for absorption to restore a more normal equilibrium. We need to start on this endeavor as quickly as possible.

Achieving this feat will require that we manage all of the variables that are within our control. We need to contain our population, because that automatically affects how much we consume. We need to control how much we consume and, more importantly, what we consume; because these factors determine how much waste we produce.

Obviously one way to deal with this problem would be for there to be a massive reduction in the human population of the planet, and there may be some who are considering such an eventuality, but it is certainly not our only option. For my part I believe in, and am most interested in, the option to create a sustainable life for roughly the population that we have today. That option is what I call The Path to A Future.

Population

We know how to control the growth of populations: increase their prosperity. This is a scientific observation, borne out in the study of every culture across the world. The sheer effort required to have and raise children means that it's only worth having more than a couple if your survival depends on it. When the prosperity of the society rises to the level where comfort in old age can be reasonably assured without relying on children, birth rates take a nosedive. Normally there is a final surge in the population, just at the time when the prosperity reaches broadly enough to reduce infant mortality and extend life expectancy, but before the cultural habit of large families has dissipated.

A rapid and broad implementation of *super-security* is vital for the successful containment of global population. The implementation must be so rapid and so effective that it has an immediate impact on birth rates. This will require a global commitment to the *super-security* of all peoples everywhere, backed by inter-state and global guarantees of solidarity.

Consumption

Total consumption is determined by individuals making individual decisions in the context of their individual circumstances. The primary tool we have, is to ensure that consumables are priced with the full weight of their externalities.

For almost every product consumed today there is an alternative with a lower planetary footprint. Loading the price of products with the cost of mitigating their planetary impact, will allow the magic of the marketplace to channel consumption into sustainably manufactured products.

The majority of energy consumed today is generated by the combustion of stored carbon fuels extracted from the earth's crust, and burned to create waste gases that are polluting our atmosphere. There is very little more of this activity that we can afford to do, so we must price energy produced in this way with loading that reflects its scarcity. That will drive increased efficiency, reduce demand and stimulate energy produced using alternative means. This will also raise the funds necessary to invest in the sustainable energy infrastructure we need going forward and *super-security* will mitigate the impact of the higher pricing on the most vulnerable populations.

Waste

Waste is the real problem that we need to tackle. It is the waste from our energy production that is polluting our atmosphere; and our waste of the energy we produce multiplies the tragedy many times over!

Greater efficiency is the most effective, most available and most rapidly deployable alternative energy source that we have. It is vital that we embark on macro efficiency initiatives in the areas of transport and buildings, but it is also essential that we free our markets so that the micro efficiencies of micro-economic activity can deliver their full rewards to consumers and the environment as soon as possible.

Enabling the rapid flourishing of micro-enterprise *super-economies* is an essential component to re-establishing the stability of our environment. This further reinforces the vital importance of the rapid introduction of *super-security* as a fundamental building block of societies across the globe.

We may not be able to prevent significant changes in the distribution of climates across the planet, but we do have the opportunity to control the extent of those changes, and their impact on our societies. If we can pull it together and use this emergency as the opportunity and the motivation to move to *super-trio* based societies living in sustainable prosperity, then we will have made something worthwhile out of what could have been a disaster.

Inter-Migration

Whether you already see it as an issue in your society today or you peer only a short distance into the future, the migration of people is a big issue, and we all need to understand how we're going to deal with it.

If you live in the richer parts of the world you call this issue "immigration", and if you live in the poorer parts of the world you call it "economic emigration". Really, it's all migration. It's all about the struggle of people to find a place in the world where they can sustain themselves and their dependents. So there are two parts to this issue:

- the assimilation of migrant populations into places that can sustain them
- the mitigation of areas so that they can sustain their populations.

To take the second one first, because it's relatively straightforward: we have to develop an awareness of the consequences of our actions, and particularly the manner in which our needs are filled. It behooves everyone to do what we can to manage the areas of land that can sustain a population, such that they continue to be able to do so. This is the heart of the environmental consequences that result from failing to manage our atmosphere; parts of our planet that can support a population today will be unable to do so in the future. But in addition to the long-term environmental damage that is already in the consequence pipeline, we continue to engage in short-term activities that further degrade our environment and cultures; turning productive land that could support a population into unsustainable areas that can't. Whether it's controlling pollution or providing technical and economic assistance, we must all do what we can to help preserve the ability for populations to remain where they are, living in sustainable prosperity.

Having said that, we already have significant migration between cultures and continents, and are likely to face even more in the future. We must have common standards and structures that allows us to accommodate migration, if we are to avoid the deep valleys of conflict that will surely consume resources, time, and probably us, if we don't.

Built into each of the three premises of The Path are the elements necessary for successful migration.

By emphasizing conflict resolution, *super-democracy* empowers people to remain in environmentally sustainable areas that would otherwise become uninhabitable because of cultural and political conflict.

Super-democracy also provides the framework within which migration can be accommodated, because it recognizes that migration is just the flow of people. In a *super-democratic* structure, migration is managed on an inter-Community level; whereby individual migrants move, with permission, from one Community to another, and are received voluntarily into their destination Community. In practice this means that communities that wish to increase their population, and have the capacity to do so, advertise the availability of residency in their Community to those wishing to migrate. The receiving Community gives specific and individual residency permission to each arriving migrant. A right which cannot be revoked, and which includes the responsibility to provide *super-security* services to the new resident.

Let's say I want to move somewhere else, to find a better job and improve my lot in life. I would look in the area I want to move to for Communities that have open residency spaces, perhaps using an online registry. I would apply to each Community and await their responses. On acceptance, I would pick the one that most appealed to me and I would move to that Community, maybe initially staying in temporary public housing until I could find work and a place of my own. The Community may have promoted the right to work to its Region, and that would allow me to take a job anywhere in the Region, although I would need to remain resident in the specific Community into which I had been accepted. My new Community might allow me citizenship after 3 years so I can vote in Community elections. The Region and State might require 5 years residency for citizenship at those layers, so my ability to vote in their elections would have to wait longer. If my migration is between two Communities in the same Transterritory, then my citizenship of the Transterritory would not be affected, and I would retain my citizenship and right to vote in the elections for that layer.

As a resident of the new Community, I have access to all the same *super-security* services that are available to everyone else in the Community. That might include healthcare, local public transport and education services. If a member of my family wishes to join me after I have moved, they would also have to apply to the Community for residency, and would be subject to the same approval process I was. If they are refused residency they can still visit me as my guests, but they are not entitled to any *super-security* services, and cannot stay for longer than a typical tourist visa allows.

While, at first glance, it might seem that the provision of *super-security* services in one society is going to provide a motivation for migration there, we need to remember the importance of congruity when building the path. Encouraging, coordinating and supporting the development of *super-security* services in all states and societies across the globe is a vital corollary to implementing the same services in our own societies.

The development and facilitation of micro-economics, as a supplement to the enterprise and industrial economy, is an important facet of the *super-economy* that mitigates migration. By enabling the emergence of the micro-economic fabric naturally inherent to human society, we not only greatly enhance the resilience of our economic structures; we also increase and improve the ability of smaller and more diverse communities to support themselves. This ability to create sustainable prosperity, without dependence on capital intensive industry, opens up large areas of perfectly sustainable land to remain as desirably inhabitable.

Apart from doing our very best to minimize and mitigate the future impacts of climate change, there is little we can do to restrain the pressures that cause migration. What we can do is reduce the need to migrate, and implement the mechanisms necessary to accommodate the migration that will happen. These are contained within the basic building blocks of The Standards of LIFE.

We should remind ourselves again that The Path does not offer a perfect solution, that not everyone will be entirely satisfied with the outcome, and it is just as important that we do the same for others as we do for ourselves. It also remains true that if we do not build The Path, we will be condemning ourselves with every action we do not take.

It's going to be hard work, but at least we have a direction to go in and an idea of where we want to get to. To that extent, we are all migrants.

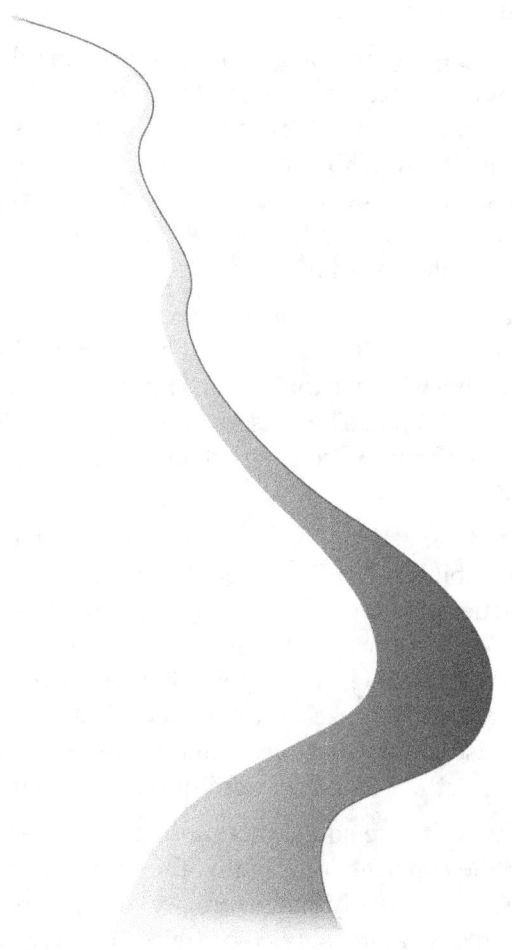

Orderly Change

Beyond the plan, the materials and the structure of The Path, there remains the greatest barrier of all: our willingness to start building it.

I'm not saying we don't want to; I'm saying that it's hard for most of us to actually *do* something before we can imagine doing it. It is the nature of the human psyche to assess risk before engaging in action. If we cannot imagine the consequences of our actions, we cannot assess the risks of taking them. This is the final barrier, my friend: to be able to *image-in* The Path, so that we can make a start on building it.

The difficulties that we all face are, I suspect, the same. We can see the value in The Path, we can understand its logic, and we can imagine where it will take us; but it is getting from here to there that's tough. The reasons are twofold: we're not sure if we can do it, and we're pretty damn sure that other people won't do it.

The first one is the easy one. We may not be confident of our own abilities but, if we could be sure of everyone else's willing participation, we know we would quite easily put aside our fears, buckle up and dig in. And therein lies the reason why this is so possible, so tangible, that we have only to reach out and grab it. Because everybody else is the same as you! Everyone else knows that they could also muster the courage to build the Path, if only they were sure of *your* participation.

And why are we so damn sure that other people will not join us in the construction? I think the first thing to recognize is that we're not actually damn sure, we're only pretty sure, and maybe even only kinda sure. We think to ourselves, "*It's those people out there, people I don't know but I've heard about who I'm pretty sure just won't be up for these kinds of changes. There are people in this world who are just too damaged; who have too much invested in the way it is now, to want to change anything.*"

Well I agree, there are some people who, for a variety of reasons, will not be there at the opening ceremony, and still others who will resist long after we have started building The Path. But this small minority is not the real barrier. We all know that it only takes some of us to get on board, and the rest will either join us or be swept along later.

No, the real barrier is our fear that the great majority of all the *good* people we know will not join us. We know they could, we know they should, but we're just not sure that they're going to. In reality they are all just the same as us. In fact they are us, and this fear is just a reflection of ourselves.

The most powerful thing we can do to stimulate our own imaginations is to walk The Path a little. Take a slow and deliberate stroll through our own personal landscape, to figure out exactly what course The Path would take in our own lives. This very intentional, conscious activity helps us develop a much clearer picture of how The Path will look. When we reach places where we assume we will meet resistance, we can look for ways around the obstacle; we may not defeat it, but maybe it does not prevent our further progress either. In working through these situations in our imaginations, we actually start to build a much more concrete picture of how it can all work. We will see that not everybody has to be on board, that not every situation has to be perfectly resolved; and we can still go forward in meaningful ways that are all steps towards our destination. The Path will not be built all at once, it will be built piece by piece and step by step, and those early sections will seem small at first, but later we will herald them as the foundations of our journey.

So join me in a slow and deliberate exploration of the evolution of The Path. This is not an illustration of how it will be in your life, or how it will be in anyone's life. It is an exercise in understanding our own assumptions and developing our own visions for change in our lives.

Walking The Path

Let's say you, or your friend, have just been elected as the mayor of a city, or the governor of a regional state, on a Standards of LIFE agenda. What's the first thing you're going to do? What does the world look like the morning after your election victory? It all looks just the same. Everything works just the way it did the day before, everyone can go about their lives – but with one important difference: they know that change is coming.

Pick three initiatives to get the ball rolling, one from each major element of the path: democratic reform, enhanced personal security and economic liberalization. By engaging in all three areas at once, you help people see the connections between them, and you leverage the reinforcing nature of The Path.

For democratic reform: you propose to devolve direct control of spending to those Communities that organize themselves to directly elect assemblies to take responsibility for the services that they wish to control. You establish an Election Commission tasked with assisting Communities to establish their boundaries, and set up their internal *super-democratic* structure. This will need to be accompanied by a census of all residents in each community. All this will take some time, require lots of education and stimulate lots of debate – all excellent consequences!

In the area of enhanced personal security you propose to adjoin the existing homeless shelter program with a free long-term housing program. The program is initially funded using part of the cash benefit stream that would otherwise have been paid to the beneficiaries, and partly by instituting a 50% local income tax for all the residents of the housing.

Introduce a law that allows for the public acquisition of private property that has been abandoned, at prices that equate to no higher than the cost of new construction for a standardized housing unit. This law would also allow for private property owners that declare bankruptcy to sell their property to the Community using the same pricing schedule.

This new housing law would allow bankrupt homeowners to stay in their houses, but will also raise howls of protest from the banking and mortgage providers. They will claim that this provision will mean that they can no longer offer mortgages to residents of the area, because any borrower can simply default on their mortgage at no risk to themselves. You can point out to them that they are perfectly entitled to sell mortgages that include personal guarantees and insurance policies. The other good news for mortgage companies is that there is now an established floor to the value of properties, should they enter foreclosure. There are in fact considerable downsides to any resident that takes advantage of the new law, because they would have to declare bankruptcy and would most likely never be able to own their own property using a loan in the future. Furthermore the occupant would now be a tenant of public housing, and subject to all of the constraints incumbent in that, such as mandatory energy efficiency and division of the property into multiple dwelling units if space allows.

To enhance the local micro-economy you launch an online services and products exchange that allows residents of your constituency to find local suppliers that can meet their needs. You work urgently with other neighboring constituencies to establish links with their online exchanges as well, using the SPEx model.

Introduce new laws that protect people's privacy both digitally and in the real world. One of these new laws will require any organization holding digital records about individuals to provide the means for those individuals to review and dispute the content of those records. Local police can be ordered to desist from any efforts or expenditures related to soft drugs, and to divert those resources into providing foot patrols at all times of the day and night. Establish a panel to review the application of all laws pertaining to the activity of an individual in their own private space; with the objective of reforming all laws from such application, and for establishing a new schedule of substances that are to be regulated according to their potential health risks.

A month after your election victory, what have you got? You've got very heated debates happening in all sorts of areas of your constituency, but the basic fabric of life for the vast majority of residents has not substantially changed. The buses still run, water still comes out of the taps and traffic wardens still write parking tickets. An understanding will be developing amongst your constituents that quite significant changes can be introduced without their lives falling apart; that these seemingly radical changes are in fact evolutionary not revolutionary.

Your second month in office: time to initiate another round of changes. Form an Election Commission to establish the framework for a directly elected, single assembly that will represent your constituency after the next election cycle, along with the start of a new constitution. This new assembly will replace all elected officials, including your own office. The new structure will only come into effect after either a referendum or the next election. In other words, begin to start the preparation for *super-democracy* at the very level of government that you are operating at; but you are not going to force it onto anybody, and you are going to give it plenty of time for organization and education.

Commission the establishment of one or more Community Centers that contain canteens that will serve meals free of charge to all residents. Target their opening for no less than one year ahead.

Use the previously announced abandoned property acquisition law to establish micro-workshop incubators in which local residents can start their own businesses.

Start the public comment period for an initiative that aims to restrict the use of petroleum powered vehicles in the central retail areas of the city. Work with the retailers to help them see that it is in their commercial interest to have consumers that want to come downtown, feel safe there and stay there for a longer period each time they come. Get the local mass transit providers involved so that they are ready to provide complementary services when the changes to the road system are made, approximately two years from now. Announce the introduction of a carbon tax on all fuel sold, starting in six months, which will be used to help fund the above changes.

All of these changes and announcements will stimulate the debate about what it really costs to provide the basic services that support our lives, so now is a great time to establish a commission to do exactly that. The commission's objective is to establish a per person cost for each of the BASE/*super-security* services (go to www.standardsoflife.com/base for more info), specific to your constituency. The commission should publish intermediate findings as they proceed, so that there can be vigorous public debate and input about what services are included and how they are provided. This research and information is a vital input to the development of true personal security and a linked income tax.

Use the rest of your first year in office working through the issues that arise, taking every opportunity to encourage and educate as the process unfolds. Encourage the debate about personal liberty so people have the chance to walk themselves through the consequences, obligations and rewards of enshrining true personal freedom into the foundation of their society.

At around your first anniversary two important processes should be culminating: the establishment of elected Community assemblies, and the determination of the costs of BASE services. Putting these two together will allow you to provide very concrete numbers, so that people can understand what it will mean to take responsibility for providing *super-security* services in their Community. This in turn will stimulate the debate inside Communities about what services they wish to retain responsibility for, and which they think they would be better off promoting up and sharing with a Regional authority.

At the end of year one you will have a clear picture of income distribution across the population. This will allow you to present specific numbers regarding the rate of income tax that will be necessary to support the BASE services, or maybe the service restrictions that will be necessary in order to stay within the bounds of a reasonable income tax. This also provides an opportunity for Communities to think about whether they will want to supplement the BASE funds they receive with local sales or property taxes, in order to deliver higher quality and/ or more extensive services.

In order to make the transition after the next election or referendum as effective and successful as possible, it is important that everybody has the opportunity to come up to speed on what their responsibilities will be, and the kinds of decisions that they will have to make. The process of establishing Communities, taking a census of residents, reviewing the costs of providing services and determining what they are better off working with others to provide and what they would rather keep responsibility for themselves, are all important for the familiarization and education of the citizenry.

As you roll into your second year it will be clear to everyone that what they are engaged in is a process of radical but orderly change; that substantial and fundamental changes can be considered, discussed, debated, planned and implemented without the disintegration of the fabric of society. As the concepts inherent to The Path become more concrete and specific, they also become easier to imagine and more personal. This familiarity breeds confidence and allows the public discourse to move from whether or not The Path should be built, to where and how The Path is going to be built.

About three years should be plenty of time for people to develop a realistic and rational perspective of the kinds of changes that are possible, and what the likely impacts will be on their lives. This is the time to call an early election, or organize a referendum, seeking the people's support for the orderly progress towards full *super-democracy*, complete personal security and a vibrant micro economy.

Campaign hard, the future of your planet depends on it!

Shovel-ready Actions

Small steps alone are just that, but small steps taken in the direction of a vision are powerful foundations for change.

We're not going to wake up one day and everything's going to be different. We're going to wake up one day and everything is going to be the same, except that we've decided to change it; decided to change some of it now, more of it later and the rest of it after that. As part of learning to visualize what that looks like, here are some stand-alone actions that we could take or advocate for as citizens.

One small step toward security would be to guarantee shelter and sustenance for a group of people. Have the government of your community buy up a few houses, renovate them with local labor and then rent them for no money to that group. Employ someone to run a kitchen and cook food given freely to that group. Then let everyone in the group do whatever they can to make money and commit to pay half of whatever they make into a fund to pay for the housing upkeep and the food. When the fund's income exceeds the cost of the housing and food, introduce additional services such as free local bus passes and vouchers that can be exchanged for classes at local educational establishments. Expand the service to more groups. Never provide cash and do not do for one what you cannot do for all.

Another small step would be to organize your community around support for a carbon tax. Run some seminars and distribute information to help people understand the importance of a carbon tax and its relative merits compared to the tinkering distractions of cap-and-trade. Then organize everyone to put concerted pressure on local, regional and national politicians to introduce such a tax.

Start collecting a carbon tax in your own community and use the funds to support local mass transport or improve building insulation. Offer to harmonize tax rates with any nearby constituencies that also adopt a carbon tax. Start small, just add 5 cents a gallon to fuel sold locally.

Get together with people in your community to support the concept of replacing all of the different local elected officials with a single assembly to which all aspects of local government, from schools to the police, will be accountable. Discuss reducing the voting age to 16, and giving a proxy vote to guardians for each of their dependents.

Close most of the roads in your town center to petro-driven vehicles and provide coin-operated electric carts for public use.

Make all public mass transport free for use in your community.

Put a GPS tracker on the roof of every public bus and link it to a web page so that everyone can see where the buses are at anytime.

Build a web site that allows everyone in your community to advertise any services or products that they make or build themselves.

Work out what it would cost to build a standard housing unit in your community and how much it would cost per person to provide a healthy diet. Publish your methodology and numbers to share with others locally and internationally.

Open the schools during the school holidays to allow anyone in the community to run a class on the subject of their choice and have that class schedule advertised on a community web site.

Introduce a local currency printed on biodegradable paper that disintegrates or expires after a year, so that it either needs to be spent or banked. Banks participating in the system can provide loans, at a 4:1 deposit ratio, if they provide parallel currency accounts for their customers.

Define the boundaries of your new Community constituency by soliciting the voluntary association of the residents. Get a map, draw a provisional boundary and go to every resident and ask them to sign a petition confirming the boundary. Explain to them that they will have to be in a Community and if not this one, then how would they draw the map?

Start a process to define what aspects of law the residents of your Community would like to be promoted or shared with other Communities in your Region. Start with a template from www.standardsoflife.org, get your local lawyers involved pro-bono to help draft the language, and share your decisions with neighboring Communities.

Find a large wall in your community that would be appropriate to use as an "Art Wall". Divide the wall into clearly marked sections and start a booking system at the local library which allows any resident to select an available section on which they can paint whatever they want. Once a month each section is photographed and posted online to a community web site and, perhaps, also added to an album in the library. After being photographed the whole wall is repainted white and the booking system restarted.

Got some more ideas? Tell others about them at *www.thepathtoafuture.com*.

Get elected!

This is a political process, a democratic process, and that means getting elected. Quite frankly, it's hard to see The Path getting built without the direct involvement and leadership of those of us living in industrialized democracies. It is in these countries that the greatest changes have to happen; so those of us concerned with creating a future must step up to the plate, and create the opportunities for change.

You may not have considered yourself a candidate for political office, but if you've read this book and you agree with the principles and the broad thrust of the practice, then you may be the most important person to run for office in your constituency. You don't need to run as a member of an existing political party, you can appeal directly to the electorate as an independent.

The Standards of LIFE (*www.standardsoflife.com*) provides you with a complete platform that is designed to provide Path-builders with a comprehensive framework on which to run for office. A ready to go, free to use, available for modification, policy platform to support your effort to win election at any level, from community to international. Use the campaign ethics described in the Standards and you will have already distinguished yourself from the other candidates.

If you think about the elements of The Path that we have discussed, and review the policies in the Standards of LIFE, I'm sure that there will be certain parts that stand out as particularly resonant to the situation and the society that you live in. Use those elements as the headlines for your campaign, focusing on the specific issues and concerns of your constituents. Voters are concerned about the small things and the big issues, so you can emphasize solutions to their immediate problems while the Standards of LIFE provides you with a comprehensive umbrella that describes where you stand on all the other issues.

Although many existing democracies are orientated around established political parties, nearly all of them provide significant opportunity for independents to stand – they recognize that it would be hard for them to legitimately call themselves democratic if they didn't. Standing as an independent frees you to speak directly to the aspirations of your constituents, and there is no one to tap you on the shoulder and tell you to get back in line. Look for elected executive offices, like those of Mayor or Governor, because they will give you more opportunity to introduce change at the same time that you advocate for the abolition of the very post you got elected to!

Keep in mind that even if you don't win your election, just the sheer fact that you got out there and advocated for change with a campaign that reached out and touched people, is a huge contribution to the process of raising awareness and developing consciousness.

If you do win, but find yourself in a minority battling against entrenched interests, don't lose heart. Even if you don't get the changes you want enacted the first time you get elected, you can spend some of your time making sure that more Path builders get elected the next time, and more voters can visualize The Path for themselves.

If you don't run for office but see someone who is, someone who is advocating for the principles of The Path and the Standards of LIFE, give them money, time and support. Let them know that you're out there, and that you believe in the same changes too. Offer an hour a week of your time to help with the campaign, hand out leaflets, stand on street corners with banners, and organize meetings where the candidates can talk about what they want to do and answer questions.

Good people working for a common purpose with a clear path of action can save the day. There are good people out here all around us, the common purpose of our prosperity is inside us, what we need now is coordinated action. This Path is a plan that creates clarity of intention, consistency of motion and unity in action.

A framework for this plan is described in the Standards of LIFE. It serves as a model for action and a platform for change. The Standards of LIFE is a unifying platform on which independents everywhere can stand for election to change the world.

The common points in your manifesto will be:

- Deliver a set of universal services for free; including at least shelter and sustenance
- Collect income taxes sufficient only to cover the cost of the universal services
- Create marketplaces for micro-enterprise
- Collect carbon and waste taxes
- Devolve power to elected Community governments
- Establish Regional, State, Transterritorial and World assemblies
- Enshrine personal freedom in law

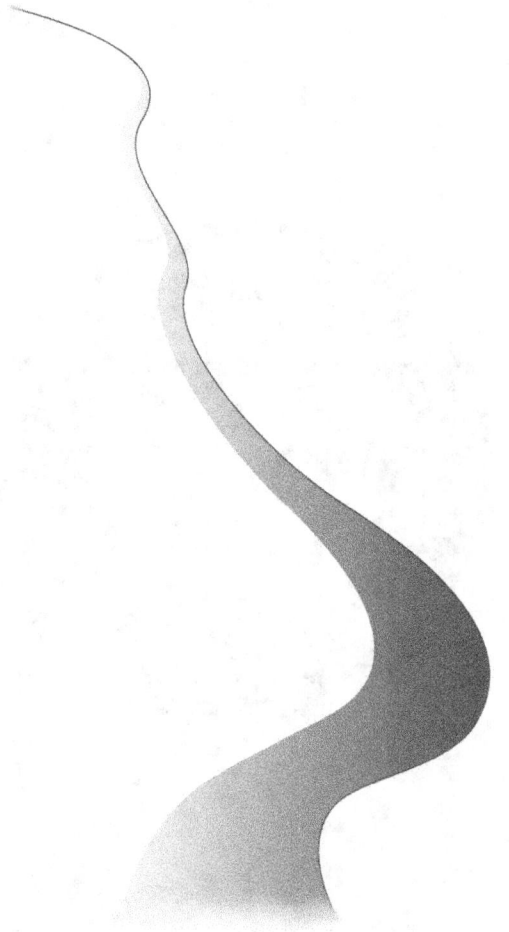

Fun, Freedom and Joy

Amidst all this talk of policies and choices, economies and democracies and the tasks that lie ahead of us, it is important to keep in touch with the joy of the moment and the happiness we seek in our destination.

This is a truly fantastic time to be alive because we are the ones that can smile in the face of all the adversity we see around us; we are the ones, the first ones ever, who can change all that. Don't lose sight of the wondrous situation that we find ourselves in, because it is our connections to our hearts that will provide us with direction when our brains are tired or confused.

The Path is a journey of joy. We are building The Path because we seek to fulfill our natural right to joyous lives filled with laughter and light, for ourselves and for everyone around us. We know that our joy cannot be sustained without the same light shining in the lives of all our fellow planet dwellers.

The journey and the destination are described by fun and freedom, not by right and wrong. Freedom and respect are the lights on The Path that illuminate the way for all to pass. If we allow shadows to fall we will lose our way, even when The Path is there. We must be mindful of according the same freedoms to others that we hold dear for ourselves, otherwise our Path will darken along with our hearts and the joy that we wish for will elude our grasp.

So smile, keep your heart out in front of you and go about your day, your work, your life with the joy of knowing that you are a Path builder with the simple intention to be one.

Fun, freedom and joy for everyone, living in sustainable prosperity, for posterity!

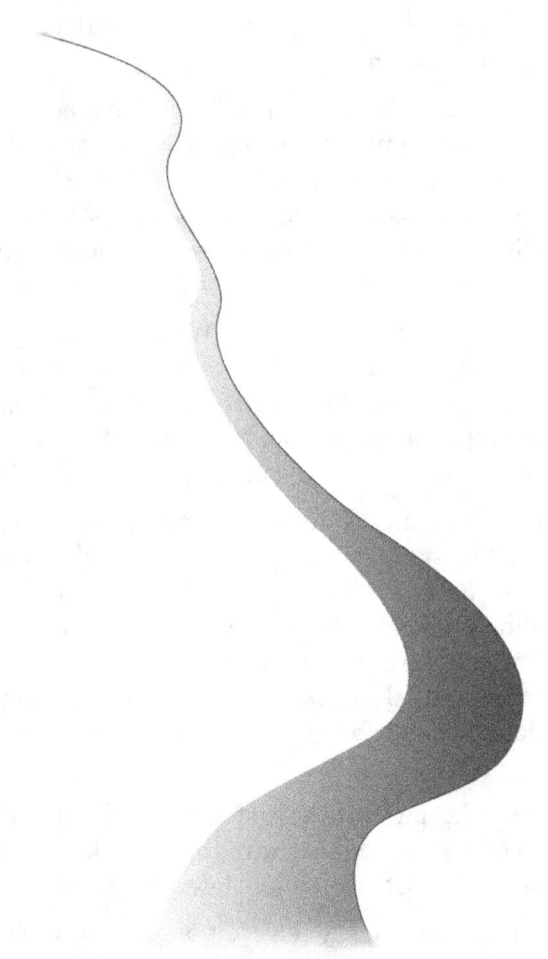

Index